Praise for *Standing Tall in a Falling World*:

'I highly recommend Angelique's book, Standing Tall in a Falling World. *From the cover, to the final page, it is so relevant! Full of insight and inspiration, this book appeals in its practicality. The format allows for easy reading in both a hectic schedule, and a leisurely lifestyle. As you read, you will be challenged, uplifted and changed!'*

Barbara Allen

'A beautiful, inspiring, transformative work. Angelique du Toit doesn't just reveal our glorious gifts she shows us how to use them. The world is a better place for her words.'

Justin Cohen, speaker, trainer, author

'Angelique has a way of stirring women up to arise and be all God created them to be! The chapters are short and make for easy reading. You cannot remain the same after immersing yourself in its pages. Men will benefit too! Angelique writes from the heart and this spills over onto its pages.'

Jenny Ward

STANDING
TALL
IN A FALLING WORLD

STANDING
TALL
IN A FALLING WORLD

ANGELIQUE DU TOIT

HAY HOUSE

Carlsbad, California • New York City • London • Sydney
Johannesburg • Vancouver • Hong Kong • New Delhi

First published and distributed in the United Kingdom by:
Hay House UK Ltd, Astley House, 33 Notting Hill Gate, London W11 3JQ
Tel: +44 (0)20 3675 2450; Fax: +44 (0)20 3675 2451; www.hayhouse.co.uk

Published and distributed in the United States of America by:
Hay House Inc., PO Box 5100, Carlsbad, CA 92018-5100
Tel: (1) 760 431 7695 or (800) 654 5126
Fax: (1) 760 431 6948 or (800) 650 5115; www.hayhouse.com

Published and distributed in Australia by:
Hay House Australia Ltd, 18/36 Ralph St, Alexandria NSW 2015
Tel: (61) 2 9669 4299; Fax: (61) 2 9669 4144; www.hayhouse.com.au

Published and distributed in the Republic of South Africa by:
Hay House SA (Pty) Ltd, PO Box 990, Witkoppen 2068
info@hayhouse.co.za; www.hayhouse.co.za

Published and distributed in India by:
Hay House Publishers India, Muskaan Complex, Plot No.3, B-2,
Vasant Kunj, New Delhi 110 070
Tel: (91) 11 4176 1620; Fax: (91) 11 4176 1630; www.hayhouse.co.in

Distributed in Canada by:
Raincoast Books, 2440 Viking Way, Richmond, B.C. V6V 1N2
Tel: (1) 604 448 7100; Fax: (1) 604 270 7161; www.raincoast.com

Text © Angelique du Toit, 2010, 2015

Previously published in 2010 by Standing Tall Publications

The moral rights of the author have been asserted.

A catalogue record for this book is available from the British Library.

ISBN: 978-1-78180-553-4

Printed and bound in Great Britain by TJ International Ltd, Padstow, Cornwall

*This book is lovingly dedicated to my mother, Joyce Lourens,
my role model and mentor, who taught me to stand
tall when everything in our world was falling.*

*Thanks Mom, for leaving me a great legacy when you passed
from this earth to live in eternal Glory on 31 May 2004.*

This book is especially in memory of you!

Contents

Contents

Foreword

Here is a rare chance to find a book that offers sound, practical advice on how to achieve one's divine destiny. My precious friend Angelique du Toit's book blends smart practice with intelligent articulation of how to get the journey started. *Standing Tall in a Falling World* is an invaluable and extraordinary book. It lays out a simple step-by-step process by which anyone can discover, pursue and achieve his or her God-given dream for life.

If you are seeking a major transformation of your life, *Standing Tall In a Falling World* will clearly show you how to get direction in times of challenge. This book is filled with encouragement and wisdom. If you are questioning your future, or you may be at a crossroads in your life or even facing a crisis… this book is for you. It will bring out the glow of hope in times of loneliness and rejection.

In this hectic day and age, the art of dreaming big and planning to reach that dream is often overwhelmed by the mundane and routine pressures of life. Therefore it is refreshing to read this inspiring book that will lift your life's passion, potential and purpose. I have no doubt that each one of us can embark on our personal dream journey and ultimately achieve it.

Angelique, you have truly given us a valuable and practical guide, a must-read for anyone who cares to stand tall in times of trouble. I am inspired to keep dreaming. This book will definitely strike a chord in every heart. I know that this book will revive people's dreams to experience uncommon favour and blessings. Everyone has a dream just ready and waiting to be fulfilled.

I recommend this book as a life manuscript for those who want to live life well, dream big and boldly possess their future.

I CAN... YOU CAN... TOGETHER WE CAN stand tall even in a falling world.

Dr David Molapo
CEO, I CAN Foundation

Introduction

The concepts in this book, *Standing Tall in a Falling World*, relate to you and to every human being, regardless of what start you have had in life, where you find yourself in your present, or where you are planning to go in your future.

This is not a book based on theory or hearsay, it is not secondhand revelation, but rather it is full of life-changing principles that are alive and that have the inherent ability to bring about quantum changes in your life, if you choose to apply them and live by them.

Life experiences at times can leave you feeling confused, fragmented, depressed and directionless. But then there is always an alternative; always another route, always the power and freedom to choose. Life is only a dead end when the end comes. Until then, you have the power of the 'Y' alternative. The 'Y' in your life is the scenario where you are travelling on the road of life only to be confronted with a situation that demands a choice. You can only go one way or the other. There is not the luxury of a 'middle road'. It is at this juncture that you win or you lose by the way you choose.

To stand tall when everything else around you is tumbling down is a choice. The call to stand tall has nothing whatsoever to do with your physical stature, or even how tall or big you try to project yourself to the outside world. Rather it is a call to stand; to stand tall on the inside, even when circumstances may be shouting at you to sit, lie down or fall down! To rise up with a shifted mindset that is unshackled from past thought patterns, self-limiting beliefs, allowing confidence to overflow everywhere you go. This is foundational to **standing tall** on the inside. **Standing tall** in your life is boosted by having your identity established and rooted in the love and acceptance of Jesus Christ, the One who came to free mankind from all that tries to keep us dwarfed forever. You can stand tall in the liberty by which Christ has made you free, and you never again have to be entangled with any yoke or bondage. You can stand tall because He has healed your broken heart, restored your self-esteem and set you free. No longer do you have to be captive to life-destroying behaviour, or crippled by oppression, depression or addiction, because where the Spirit of the Lord is, there is liberty – freedom – joy! This is the time to live free from your past, to live abundantly in the present and with great expectation for a glorious future. This liberty is there for you. Make the choice to stand tall today even if it seems that everything in your world is falling!

How to Get Real Benefit from Reading this Book

Standing Tall in a Falling World has been written for more than just your reading pleasure. It has been designed for you to get real-time, daily benefit from applying the power-packed principles in your life.

The easy-to-read, conversational style of writing enables you to enjoy a number of benefits from this book:

1. Ideally, find a quiet space and place – alone – and allow the words to sink deep into your soul. Create some 'me' time, a time of introspection and reflection. Keep a pen and a highlighter close by so you can mark the concepts and words that light a flame in you. Be sure to make your own notes in the 'Reflection' space provided at the end of each chapter. Writing is therapeutic and healing, it is revelational and directional. Make the most of the time you owe to yourself. Don't rush through it – meditate, contemplate and reflect – take your time and most of all – enjoy it!

2. You may choose to read the book through once, as one would read a novel. Then go back and take the time to take ownership of what you have read and commit yourself to apply that which you know you need to make a difference to your life.

3. If the only 'me' time you can give yourself is 'here-and-there', pick up the book and find the chapter that relates to your current need. The chapters are short enough to read while stirring the pot on the stove, while your baby is napping, or during a tea or lunch break at the office. When you move on to your next task, let the content be your constant companion as you decide where to apply the truths that can change your life.

4. If you are really on the run, sneak a peek at the Scriptures or the quotations and inspire yourself for the day. Words can change your world. One sentence can shine like a very bright light in a very dark place. Possibility is only one sentence away. One word can be the beginning of a new world for you. Stop… breathe… listen… you may be very surprised at how much and what you hear! Don't allow the pace of the world to rob you of your personal opportunity to stand tall!

Chapter One

Standing Tall in Your Soul

S oul – Your soul is that part of you that consists of your mind, your will, your emotions and your conscience. It is the place where your character is formed and your memory bank is stored, and it is the seat of your emotions and your feelings. Your personality is a reflection of the state of your soul.

Your soul is alive from the moment you are conceived and therefore every experience from birth to the present day has made an impact, and left its mark on your soul. You are the sum total today of your experiences, your thoughts and your actions of yesterday.

The good news is this: whatever you have personally experienced in your soul, whatever may be plaguing your conscience, or regardless of what may appear to be holding you back from **standing tall**, you can change and shift all of this today! Your soul was magnificently created to live in freedom, in joy, in fruitfulness and in abundance. The destiny of your soul lies in the choices you make on a moment-by-moment basis. You decide whether you shackle your soul with destructive thinking, guilt, anger or depressing actions. The fabulous alternative is that you can choose to receive the forgiveness that Jesus came to give you and know His freedom in your mind, in your will and in your emotions, and live with a conscience that does not condemn you. Your soul's transformation is one choice away.

A Personal Sense of Purpose ❧

You have gifts, talents and experiences that only you can release to take you to the place you ought to be. Your purpose drives your passion so you can powerfully fulfil your personal calling.

Your purpose, though you may not know it, is that desire or imagination that stirs, excites and ignites you. It is often the seemingly impossible, that which seems so far removed from where you find yourself in the present. Your personal purpose gives you the opportunity to break out of your self-limiting beliefs and opens your heart wide to embrace that for which you were so purposefully created. 'But how is one to find one's true place in life?' you might ask.

Multitudes of people meander through life wondering if there is a real purpose to their life. Where do you even begin to discover what God created and birthed you for? You may even look at your life with a certain cynicism, often tempted to focus on what you don't have instead of noticing what is a potential gift in you. Your negative self-talk may have caused you to miss some sterling opportunities.

But if you will take a moment, find some solitude in the busyness of your world and reflect on how many times you have felt a resonating on the inside of you at an exciting possibility ahead, and the times you have felt and seen many clues that were strewn across your path, you may just be tapping into that very substance of your heart's desire. In the words of Emmet Fox: '…already in your past life from time to time, God Himself has whispered into your heart just that very wonderful thing, whatever it is, that He is wishing you to be and to do, and to have. And that wonderful thing is nothing less than what is called YOUR HEART'S DESIRE.'

Embrace your heart's desire because it is God who put it there. God has foreordained your future and He has already empowered you to make it happen. Your desire is your blueprint. His personal plan for you is no carbon copy. Your purpose for living your life is almost always aligned with what you really want to do more than anything else. It is for this reason that some people yearn to be surgeons and yet the girl next

2

door faints at the sight of a drop of blood. Or why an astronaut can be physically and mentally equipped to go through the gruelling tests that enable him to head out into space, and why someone like me would be sidelined on day one for motion sickness in the extreme. Living a purpose-filled life starts with finding out what comes naturally to you. Ask yourself why you want to do something specific or significant. Don't waste another moment of your life wishing you could be like someone else. Proverbs 18:16 declares that, *'A gift gets attention; it buys the attention of eminent people.'* God put your gifts in you before you were born. Your gifts have shaped your personality and can shape your future if you will allow them to surface and be seen, and be experienced by others. Your unique gifts are designed in your DNA. Your past experiences have been preparing you for your future. Experiencing the fulfilment of your personal calling may be closer than you believe. Your beginnings are not a reflection of your destiny.

Whenever I reflect on a life that was full of experience, hidden and prepared in a secret place, only to be released when the time was right, the life of Moses is a great reminder of how God plans our lives from the time of our birth to the day we depart this earth. When Moses' mother birthed him, she saw that there was something so special about him that she hid him in the reeds to save him from being killed by Pharaoh's soldiers. But as God would not have His long-term plan thwarted by anyone, the little baby was found by Pharaoh's daughter, who took him into the palace only to have his own mother nurse him! When God makes plans, they are always grand plans! He was called Moses, which means 'Pulled Out'. Moses was saved for a purpose. If you want to know if you still have a purpose on this earth, just look at yourself in the mirror and say, 'I still have a heartbeat, therefore I am here for a really good reason and a very useful purpose. I may not understand the whole picture yet, but that's okay. Neither did Moses.'

'For I know the plans I have for you,' declares the LORD. 'Plans to prosper you and not to harm you, plans to give you hope and a future.'

(JEREMIAH 29:11)

3

Little did Moses know that he was being raised and educated in Pharaoh's palace and kingdom, because one day his purpose would be to return to Egypt as God's representative and authority to decimate the political system of the day as a 'rod' in God's hands to deliver God's people! But not without first committing murder, fleeing in terror and landing up in isolation in a land called Midian. Do you find yourself in isolation right now, wondering if God has forgotten that you even exist? Are you often thinking about the once fiery dreams you held on to that now seem to be nothing more than a mirage? Or perhaps you have felt a leading, a stirring, a calling just like Moses did when God appeared to him, but find yourself back-tracking, trying to find an escape route because you don't feel ready, worthy or courageous enough?

Exodus chapter 3 is a wonderful portion of Scripture that is an encouragement when we want to find all the excuses as to why God should choose someone else through whom to fulfil His particular purpose.

> *'"I am sending you to Pharaoh to bring my people, the People of Israel, out of Egypt." Moses answered God, "But why me? What makes you think that I could ever go to Pharaoh and lead the children of Israel out of Egypt?" "I'll be with you," God said.'*
> (EXODUS 3:1–12)

When God is with you nothing shall ever, ever be impossible for you. God's final instruction to Moses was,

> *'...when you leave, you won't leave empty-handed. Each woman will ask her neighbour and any guests in her house for objects of silver and gold and jewellery and extra clothes; you'll put them on your sons and daughters. Oh, you'll clean the Egyptians out!'*
> (EXODUS 3:21,22)

Egypt was a place of darkness for the Israelites, but out of that darkness emerged treasures that became Israel's reward for following God out of darkness and into the land flowing with milk and honey. Your talents are your treasures – they are hidden in the secret places of your life.

Sometimes they are shut behind bars of iron – your resistant will, resulting from years of disappointment because of delay. If you will be obedient and courageous and offer those treasures to God for His plan and purpose, even as Moses did, your reward will be exceedingly great.

> *'I will go before you and make the crooked places straight;*
> *I will break in pieces the gates of bronze and cut the bars*
> *of iron. I will give you the treasures of darkness and hidden*
> *riches of secret places, that you may know that I, the Lord,*
> *Who call you by your name, Am the God of Israel.'*
> (ISAIAH 45:2,3)

God will fulfil the desire that He puts in your heart. God is dedicated to every detail of your life. Our responsibility is to prepare ourselves in every way, spiritually and practically. We plan the way we want to live, but only God makes us able to live it. (Proverbs 16:9). When you are faithful in the daily responsibilities of your life, God can entrust you with His Kingdom responsibilities. When you serve your spouse and family well, you then can be entrusted to serve others well. If the Gospel, the Good News of Jesus Christ, is not being represented by you in your home, it is not going to be well represented elsewhere. Whatever your hand finds to do, do it with all of your might. Do it as unto the Lord. Do whatever you can in preparation for His grand purpose to be released in you.

That stirring deep within your soul is the dawning of your purpose.

If you need to study more, then study. If it is to make right with someone, do so. If it is to get back to God and return from your wanderings in the wilderness, there is no better time than the present. God will not take you beyond your last step of obedience. In times of personal challenge remember that adversities make you spiritually sharp and you become more resourceful to fulfil your personal calling. The greatest place you can abide is in His Presence. So, like Moses, you know the Voice of God that is saying to you personally, 'I'll be with you always.'

God's invitation to you today is to live your life on purpose! You were created for abundance, not redundance. To live a life of action and not one in traction. To pursue your God-given passion and not merely live for your pension.

Sadly many people have had others' opinions and their own life's circumstances dictate a message that they were never meant to live a life of purpose. For others, the litany of rejections and the resultant view of themselves have deterred them from even getting off the starting block to live a life of purpose. For most, living life on purpose is just a hazy dream that surfaces from time to time, but deep roots of low self-esteem ask the question, 'How can something out-of-the-ordinary, meaningful and powerful be accomplished by me?' Yet the answer is found in the very core of the question. The answer lies in the desire that blazes like an inferno in your heart. The fact that you are asking the question gives credence to the truth that, buried under the debris of your soul, is the desire to live a life of powerful purpose.

You must embrace your heart's desire, because it is God, the One Who created you, who put that desire there. When you lose touch with the desire to live a life of purpose and meaning, you abandon your own heart. All that is left is an aching void and a continual bombardment of thoughts in your mind centring on the fact that there must be more to life than what is currently being experienced. That stirring deep within your soul is the dawning of your very own life of purpose. God has foreordained your future and He has already empowered you to make it happen. Your desire is your blueprint. The plan for your life is an original and not a carbon copy.

Your gifts are God-given. Your gifts have shaped your personality and will create your future. Your unique gifts are designed in your very DNA. Your gifts are embedded in you so that you will release them to create an avenue for revenue. Your gifts are certainly designed to become your greatest source of wealth. You just need to look at the artists, writers, musicians, fashion designers, doctors, businesspeople, speakers and actors whose gifts have been connected with purpose and passion to create their wealth and a great measure of fulfilment.

Experiencing the fulfilment of your predetermined purpose may be closer than you believe. Your beginnings are never a reflection of your destiny. Past experiences have been preparing you for your creative future. Despite the challenges of your past, fulfilling your purpose must be grounded in the knowledge that you can make a difference in the life of another. Purpose begins when you start to invest your life into the lives of others. You need to make up your mind to be a meaning-maker in this one precious life.

Knowing that you can live in the fulfilment of having a personal, powerful purpose, should inspire you to revisit your life and be liberated to dream again. Often the harsh and demanding realities of life keep you task-bound and you forget that there is a grander and more noble purpose for you to fulfil. Your purpose is already on the inside of you – you just have to take the risk, that step of faith – and release it, live in it, and enjoy it! Having purpose locked up on the inside is like having a masterpiece hidden in the cellar. Its true reason for creation will never be experienced until the masterpiece is revealed and can be enjoyed. The joyous fulfilment is found when you are living your life on purpose. Purpose starts in your heart through the actions of your hands. Arise, stand tall and shine and let your purpose be known to the world.

My Reflections on Living My Life with Purpose

✧ When are you going to emerge in the fullness of what you were purposed to be? What are you waiting for?

✧ What responsibility do you need to take to prepare yourself for your future?

✧ If God appeared to you visually as He did to Moses, what would you change in order to fulfil His call? Remember that when the time to perform comes, the time to prepare has passed!

Impact Your World ❧

SURE, SOMEDAY YOU'LL CHANGE THE WORLD. WELCOME TO SOMEDAY!

Your world. What does it look like? Who is in your world? What makes your world go round? You have been shaped by your environment. Who your parents are, your siblings, your school experiences, the people of authority in your life and your own personal choices have all formed your world. Your choices of whom you associate with, where you work and apply your skills, your relationships, and how you spend your time also create your world. What does your world feel like to you? Does it give you negative or positive feedback? Is your world adding value to your life or is it detracting from your life? Are you **standing tall** in your world or is your world falling in on you?

Jonathan Edwards was a man whom God effectively used in the Great Awakening Revival. The story of this man's approach to changing his world is a very interesting one. Jonathan Edwards prayed to God as he stood on the riverbank, crying out for revival in the land and asking God to bring needed change to the city, to the region and to his nation. He then bent down and drew a circle in the sand, believing that in order for God to answer his prayer, it had to start somewhere. He then stepped into the circle, and said, 'Here I am God. Start with me.' Before you can impact your world, God has to start with you. Personal transformation is always the starting place for change. Transformation starts in the heart of the individual who in turn can influence their family and their community, which can affect the city and then ultimately a shift can take place in their nation. While everyone complains about what is not taking place in their city, nothing will change. When one steps up to the plate and says, 'Here I am Lord, use me,' that person becomes a catalyst for change.

> *You can choose to use your pain to bless or to curse; to hurt or to heal. The choice is yours.*

In our world we can use either the magnifying glass or the mirror. The magnifying glass is to see the faults of others. The mirror is to come face to face with ourselves and to ask the question – 'What do I need to change?'

Are you tired of your old world? Well, it may be that today you will make a choice to change, to stand tall and allow your life to impact your world. I know your world has negatively impacted you. It happens to all of us. But you can choose to use your pain to bless or to curse; to hurt or to heal. Whichever you choose, you will live with the fruit that is borne out of your choice. It is not the will that is central to life, it is your heart. The thoughts and intents of your heart shape every aspect of your life. What goes on in your heart will affect your world. We need to allow God to excavate the deep recesses of our lives and clear away the clutter so that He can be expressed through us. Making a choice to stand tall over anger for hurts done to you, and extending forgiveness to those who have harmed you, releases great grace into your life. When grace can't be released, you stay in pain, bowed low, ever-burdened by the weight of others' wrongs. We need God's grace in our lives. God's grace is His favour, His attractiveness, His hand extended towards us, enabling us to stand very tall.

When we walk and live in God's grace, with His DNA imprinted in us, (His Divine Nature Attributes), we can begin to impact our world.

Grace is living in God's DNA. His Divine Nature Attributes.

Whatever needs changing in your life and in your world has to start with you. If you are going to wait for someone else to change before you change, you might wait your entire life. When you hinge your life on someone else's choices, your ability to positively impact someone else's life is diminished. Your life must be grounded in God's will and plan for you to be able to impact your world with confidence. The meaning of the word impact is to have a strong effect or an impression on someone. On our own we may be able to impact someone's life for a moment, or even for a while longer, but when God is alive in us, living in and speaking through us, we can impact someone's life for a lifetime. The changes that you seek in your own world are going to start with you. The degree to which you want to impact your world (your children, your partner, your extended family, your staff or colleagues, etc.), will be the degree to which you will need to change and make choices that will give you a valuable return. If you are waiting for something to happen before you can make a greater impact, just remember that what you don't use or give away becomes wasted. What you don't use you lose. The more you use or give away, the more space you make to receive. If you don't put to use what you already have, you are unlikely to attain more. Use what you have to bless others and watch what is returned to you. What have you got to give others that could seriously impact your world in return? You can be a world-shaper, an environment-changer and a difference-maker. It's all up to you.

As one person I cannot change the world, but I can change the world of one person.

PAUL SHANE SPEAR

Choose not to live a life dictated by the environment that is pressing in around you. Live a life of focus and faith despite the conditions and challenges that surround you. Don't live in the revelation of yesterday. God is ever creating. What He creates is good in His sight. Rise up above the circumstances, past and present, overcome mediocrity and live in God's creativity. Other people may think you are very ordinary, but don't make that same mistake. You are handcrafted by the Master Sculptor. He has made you with every detail perfectly in line with His purpose for you. There is nothing about you that is there by accident – He has a way of working all things together for your good. God will use every ounce of what you surrender to Him.

My Reflections on Impacting My World

✧ What one thing can you do today that you know will make a change and give you a great return?

....

....

....

....

....

....

....

....

....

....

....

....

....

....

....

....

....

....

....

....

The Journey of Life

Do not undermine your worth by comparing yourself with others.
It is because we are different that each of us is special.

Do not set your goals by what other people deem important.
Only you know what is best for you.

Do not take for granted the things closest to your heart.
Cling to them as you would your life,
For without them, life is meaningless.

Do not let your life slip through your fingers
by living in the past nor the future.
By living your life one day at a time, you live all the days of your life.

Do not give up when you still have something to give.
Nothing is really over until the moment you stop trying.
It is a fragile thread that binds us to each other.

Do not be afraid to encounter risks.
It is by taking chances that we learn how to be brave.

Do not shut love out of your life by saying it is impossible to find.
The quickest way to receive love is to give love;
The fastest way to lose love is to hold it too tightly.
In addition, the best way to keep love is to give it wings.

Do not dismiss your dreams,
As to be without dreams is to be without hope,
To be without hope is to be without purpose.

Do not run through life so fast that you forget not only
Where you have been but also where you are going.
Life is not a race,
But a journey to be savoured each step of the way.

AUTHOR UNKNOWN

My Reflections on the Journey of Life

Soundness of Heart ❧

'A SOUND HEART IS LIFE TO THE BODY.'
(PROVERBS 14:30)

Are you really enjoying your life? Are you embracing the goodness that every day brings or lamenting that your life is not what it could be? As I slowly began to gain insight into the truth of how God sees me, loves me and cares for me, I dared to venture out of the hallway of distorted mirrors that had been the way I had lived for many years. A life of believing a lie that I wasn't worthy; that I couldn't succeed, that I didn't have much to offer, along with all the other deceptions, caused severe distortion to myself and to my strategy for life. This resulted in my wearing a mask and portraying a person to the world that really wasn't me at all. As my heart healed and I dared to believe that there was more to my life, I began to exchange all the lies for the truth of God's opinion of me. Instead of seeing myself disjointed, broken and disconnected, His image of me progressively became my reality. Beginning to live the life that God wants for you will bring forth a new enjoyment of life. He will allow you to experience abundance previously unknown and you will know the joy that overflows from a sound heart.

The perceptions you hold about your life are far stronger influences in your life than you would believe. The journey towards wholeness means that you need to challenge your perceptions, your mindsets, and your belief systems that have been established over many years by yourself, by others and by your experiences. Your environment has shaped you and what you have been taught will have infiltrated the way you see things, the way you handle matters, your opinions, your lifestyle choices and your view of God. All the decisions you make based on your perceptions will design the life you will be living for the rest of your years. For

Understanding is the wellspring of life.

instance, if you have experienced dishonesty or betrayal by a close friend or partner, the pain associated with that can cause you to live in the wrong perception that you can never trust anyone again because they will all be dishonest or betray you. You can imagine how this deceptive belief, if entrenched in your heart and mind, will seriously damage all your potential relationships whether personally, socially or professionally. It is these strongholds that need to be brought into the light of God's truth so that you can make the exchange from believing the lie to living in the truth. Believing His truth gives you peace and soundness of heart.

Transformation (Divine Exchange) is one of the processes to reach wholeness.

Transformation (Divine Exchange) is the process to reach wholeness. Divine Exchange is exchanging His truth for the lies that you have believed. Dramatically changing your thoughts, your will and your emotions, to align with how you really want to live your life, is going to require changing from the inside out. To shift anything in your life is a personal choice. To change from within requires God's assistance, it requires that Divine Exchange – exchanging the lie for the truth. It is God Who gives us new eyes with which to see. There have no doubt been many times when you wondered if you would ever see through the haze and fog; it seems that those mists surrounding your life would never dissipate. But God can and does bring clarity from the blur. Your perceptions can become sharp, clear and unclouded. Living life in wholeness becomes your reality when you start to see things differently, say things differently and allow Him to change your perceptions about everyday life. A sound heart is life to the body. A wholesome tongue is a tree of life. A tranquil mind aids good physical health; attitude and health are inextricably related. You cannot hope to grow into the likeness of Jesus Christ without being in a state of constant transformation – moving towards soundness of heart; wholeness found in the abundant life Jesus Christ came to give you.

Personal transformation is costly. The price is well worth paying because the rewards far outweigh the investment. Imagine living a life of true freedom – freedom from your past, freedom from others' opinions, free to be you. Imagine being able to look honestly at yourself in the mirror and thank God for making you just the way you are; then co-operating with Him to make the adjustments, improvements and changes necessary to release even greater joy in your life. In that place of wholeness and soundness of heart, you can thoroughly enjoy sharing your life with someone else and not be afraid of intimacy, rejection or disappointment. In that place of wholeness you may, once again, experience rejection or disappointment, but you will never again be broken by it. Your soundness is founded and grounded in God and not in man because there is no instability or shadow of turning with Him. You can totally trust the character of God. He will never let you down. You can be secure in Him. He may do things differently to your way of thinking, but He is always trustworthy and is constantly interested in your wellbeing. Trust God to bring good out of your present sufferings and then when you look back and connect the dots, you will know for certain that God has been involved in working all things together for your good. Make the choice today to put your life in God's very capable hands. To stand tall in a falling world means you acknowledge that God always knows what is best for you. You're worth it and He knows it, that's why He wants you to have it. He came that you might enjoy the whole of life; the whole loaf, not just the bread crumbs. To be sound means to be secure. Soundness and security are wonderfully connected.

You can totally trust the character of God.

My Reflections on My Soundness of Heart

✧ Soundness of heart, wholeness and His abundant life are yours for the receiving. Why not accept God's offer right now and make that Divine Exchange?

Keep Your Tongue Prisoner so Your Life can be Free ✄

'WORDS SATISFY THE MIND AS MUCH AS FRUIT DOES THE STOMACH; GOOD TALK IS AS GRATIFYING AS A GOOD HARVEST.'
(PROVERBS 18:20)

Words are amongst the most powerful forces in the universe. Wars are started over words. Words destroy or build up. Words create or desecrate. Genesis chapter one reveals the creation of the universe including our world and it all starts with… And God said. It was all in God's imagination and thought life long before it manifested as creation by His Words. Words start in your thoughts. If you don't filter your thoughts, your words spill out of your mouth before you even have a chance to apprehend them. The person who knows what and how to say something is a highly empowered person.

> 'A man of knowledge uses words with restraint, and a man of understanding is even-tempered. Even a fool is thought wise if he keeps silent, and discerning if he holds his tongue.'
> (PROVERBS 17:27,28)

Your words. If they do not add value, but rather devalue, why speak them? Silence is a great weapon; a weapon you may well need as a defence against someone else's hostility. Silently standing on what you believe is often more effective than speaking what you believe. Your silence throws your enemies into total confusion. I have made it my goal in this one life I have, to be able to say along with the Apostle Paul, 'None of these things move me.' In other words, I want to be at the place of such self-control under the direction and guidance of the Holy Spirit, that nothing has the power to cause me to react. I choose rather by God's grace to respond in maturity, wisdom and authority. Your thought life and words should be under your constant surveillance. More marriages are saved by what has not been said than this world dreams of. I believe it to be true. When another person can cause you to react recklessly and emotionally, they have power of your life!

Words are used as protective mechanisms. Words create the world in which you live. Words create wounds. Until you really understand how powerful your words are, you will have to live through the aftermath of words spoken without thought. Countless people to whom I have spoken admit that their homes are in confusion, and their relationships are in chaos because of the destructive power of the words they have spoken. Your words either build up or tear down – there is not the luxury of a third option. There is a pivotal instruction in the Bible for women when it comes to keeping the home in equilibrium and peace. This is sound advice in learning how to diffuse a situation with your husband.

Words create your world.

'So that even if any [of your husbands] do not obey the Word of God, they may be won over not by discussion but by the godly lives of their wives.'
(1 PETER 3:1B)

This is more easily read than practised but the results are well worth the practice!

Whatever is true, whatever is honourable, whatever is right, whatever is pure, whatever is lovely, whatever is of good report, if there is any excellence and if anything worthy of praise, let your mind dwell on these things.
(PHILIPPIANS 4:8)

'It is not hard to make decisions when you know what your values are.'
ROY DISNEY

Publilius Syrus was recorded in the 18th century to have said, 'I often regret that I have spoken; but never that I have been silent. Speech is the mirror of the soul.' Your words give the outside world an inside view of what is taking place in your soul.

Leonard Ravenhill said that the tongue should be kept between our teeth. We should think twice before we speak once. He exhorted his readers to keep their tongue prisoner so that their bodies could go free. Let us season our words with salt, not pepper. The tongue is indeed the index of the heart. In this 21st century, man has incredible power over this world, yet he has still not conquered his tongue. Let us speak life and not death over our lives and over our circumstances. Your words create a life of magnificence or madness. Your words can keep you in a pit or they can take you to the palace.

Every relationship knows the ecstasy of first love. However, when that ecstasy is confronted with the reality of daily living, you are faced with a choice. You can either choose words that create restoration or bring destruction. If you choose destruction, chances are you will never find ecstasy in that relationship again. Should you choose the restoration route, you can move beyond the reality to ecstasy again. Why live as inmates when you can enjoy intimacy?

Why live as inmates when you can enjoy intimacy?

Have you noticed that you don't need to tell your partner you are angry? They can sense it at the front door. You are always communicating. Your words merely confirm what you are already thinking. Your body language, your eyes, your stance, your movement and your facial expressions all tell your story before you have uttered a word. Whatever controls your mind has you. Whoever can cause you to react has power over your life. Whoever rents space in your mind is controlling your life. It's a good idea that you start thinking about what you want, not about what you don't want in your life, because your thoughts become like magnets and attract to you the very things you are thinking about, especially when you add your voice to it. Who said sticks and stones could break your bones but words would never harm you? Your words create a life of strife or a life of peace. To control your tongue is to control your life.

My Reflections on the Words of My Mouth

❖ Commit yourself to think before you speak. It could save you from a life of strife.

❖ Value your words for they give direction to your life.

Help, My Box is Full! ✍

Many times in my mailings to my networks, I receive messages in return saying that my mail could not reach the recipient because 'their box is full'. This always reminds me of a special friend of mine who, while journeying through her own process to Stand Tall, would often comment that her 'box was too full'. Whether it was emotional pain, the demands of her career as a businesswoman or her challenging relationships, the fact remained that her box was simply too full for her to live the life that she was so magnificently designed to live. I am happy to say her mailbox is now free-flowing!

When your box is too full the message is clear. You quite simply cannot receive anything more; good, bad, inspirational or indifferent. It is a clear message to you that it is time to de-clutter, to make way for something new, to revamp and restore and to empty yourself of those things that are clogging you up. The state

The state of being too full is indicative of information overload!

of being too full is indicative of information overload; of having taken in or taken on too much and you are buckling under the weight of it all. When you are burdened and weighed down, there is no way you can journey through life with a light heart, a skip in your step and a smile on your face. The very weight of your box being stuffed with undesirable memories, toxic emotions, guilt, regrets, resentments, judgements, bitterness and anger will cause you to buckle and be bent over just trying to survive life.

So how do you go about emptying your inbox? Decide what you want in your life and what you don't want in your life. Make a list across two columns. Ask yourself what you want in your inbox, i.e. those things that would make your life more abundant, happier, joyful, successful, peaceful and other life-giving attributes, and then what things should be sent to your 'outbox', ready for despatch out of your life. Once you have thoroughly evaluated and explored these questions with honesty, you need to take some action. Be mindful, however, that you cannot push the send button and hope that people will be despatched out of your life. A far more effective way of getting the desired results is to work on yourself first. Your best results are going to be experienced when you make the decision to take total responsibility for your life. No more blame-shifting, no victim approach to life, and certainly no adopting a Doris Day theory of 'whatever will be will be!' What elements of your character, your way of thinking, your habits, your weaknesses and other traits are causing your box to be too full? Excavate the areas that may have long been hidden and yet have been dangerously undermining your life such as:

- The effects of disappointments and disillusionments you have experienced and how they have negatively impacted your view of life.

- Are you constantly making excuses to avoid making changes to your life? Excuses, by the way, are neatly packaged lies that you tell yourself and others.

- How much time do you spend complaining, criticizing and condemning people and situations and this in turn works against you?

- Negative thinking, talking, and acting out what you believe may be causing destructive results in your life.

- Laziness and lack of productivity causing frustration and debt.

When you don't leave a situation in victory, it is very difficult to enter a new season in victory.

Having started the process of de-cluttering your life, don't stop! Continue working through this process and gain new territory each day. When you leave a situation in defeat, it is very difficult to enter a new season in victory. When you don't make peace with your past and despatch it out of your life, your present and your future will give you a 'sending failed' message. You will not be able to make effective progress. It is interesting to note that the word resentment, which is rooted in anger, is an emotion that, left unresolved, will cause the consequence to be 're-sent' back to you. You can live your life with resignation and anger or with purpose and possibility. Life is too short to live life with a 'system shutdown' or, more seriously, when you receive the message that a 'fatal error has occurred'.

Starting the process of clearing out your inbox today means you could have a different outcome as early as tomorrow. Just imagine the possibilities that will present themselves when you read your mail with honesty and acknowledgement. When you begin to catch a glimpse of the life that God has prepared for you and see that you were meant to be free and effective, the task of busting out of your box becomes one of purpose and determination. Why stay depressed, oppressed, bent over, hungover and disillusioned when the choice to change is a moment away? Your very next thought can be a decision to change and to declare that there is a much greater life awaiting you than the one you have settled for. Living your life with clear thinking, purpose, and excellence in all you do is sure to build your levels of confidence. To have confidence is to live with faith. To live with faith is very pleasing to God.

> *You can't have a better tomorrow if you are thinking about yesterday all the time.*
> CHARLES F. KETTERING

'There are two primary choices in life; to accept conditions as they exist, or accept the responsibility for changing them.'
DENIS WAITLEY

My Reflections on My Life's Inbox

Guilt Free! ✍

To know Him and to make His Presence known. This is the desire of my heart. The Presence of God is the environment from which we should emerge. His Presence and work in our lives is the only true foundation for our effective and lasting transformation. It is only when we consciously choose to spend our lives with Him that we begin to be changed into His likeness. Having a quality relationship with any person of significance is built by spending quality time together. In these days of incessant demands and constricting time schedules, it takes conscious thought and choice to bring God into every aspect of daily life. Not many of us have hours to spend in solitary prayer time, where we can switch off from the world and its buzz of activities, but we can make a point of giving the best part of ourselves to God every day. For some it may mean early in the morning, for others mid-morning when your spouse and children have left for the day or when you retreat at night, drawing away from the clamour of demands that constantly compete for your attention. It is who we become when we spend time in God's Presence that we should represent in all of our relationships.

Your relationship with your Heavenly Father, through Jesus His Son, is the most fundamental of all your relationships. If God is not the cornerstone in your life, the foundation on which you build your other relationships will be shaky. What I love about living life with God is that we are set free from pseudo-guilt; always feeling burdened by what we are not, because in Him we are free to enjoy the very life He gave us. We can get past the guilt of feeling that we never have enough time for Him and invite God into the 24 hours a day that we do have, committing all of our activities and facets of life to Him, asking

We therefore become the obstacle to enjoying an extravagant relationship with God because our lives are guilt-ridden and not God-driven.

Him in a practical way to be with us as we go through what is often the routine and mundane duties of the day. False guilt stems from not really believing that we deserve the best God has for us, or that we are not good enough to receive what He is offering. We therefore become the obstacle to enjoying an extravagant relationship with God because our lives are guilt-ridden and not God-driven. The one and only way to be guilt-free forever is to, without question and in total faith, even though you may not have the full understanding of what Jesus did for you on Calvary, accept the absolute fact that His sinless, pure and perfect life was given in exchange for your less-than-perfect, sin-filled, impure life.

> 'If we claim that we experience a shared life with Him and continue to stumble around in the dark, we're obviously lying through our teeth – we're not living what we claim. But if we walk in the light, God Himself being the light, we also experience a shared life with one another, as the sacrificed Blood of Jesus, God's Son, purges all our sin. If we claim that we're free of sin, we're only fooling ourselves. A claim like that is errant nonsense. On the other hand, if we admit our sins – make a clean breast of them – He won't let us down; He'll forgive our sins and purge us of all wrongdoing. If we claim that we've never sinned, we out-and-out contradict God – make a liar out of Him. A claim like that only shows off our ignorance of God.'
>
> (1 JOHN 1:6–10)

When you grasp the fact that when God the Father looks at you, He sees the beauty of His Son's atonement for and upon you, you must realize that there is nothing more you can add or do to be pleasing to God.

> 'It's impossible to please God apart from faith. And why? Because anyone who wants to approach God must believe both that He exists and that He cares enough to respond to those who seek Him.'
>
> (HEBREWS 11:6)

Until you accept by faith what Jesus has accomplished for you in this life and for eternity, God cannot be pleased since He cannot lavish on you what He desires. Yes, it is that simple. God desires more for you than you desire for yourself. Don't let your guilt, your reasoning, your intellectualism, your regret or any other negative thought or life pattern stop you from accepting His very best gift for you – personally. Take it today. It's yours – with His love and blessing.

Pursuing a deep, life-changing relationship with God is the platform for being in quality and transparent relationship with ourself. We have to make a decision to walk in the light as He is in the light.

> *'I am Light that has come into the world so that all who*
> *believe in me won't have to stay any longer in the dark.'*
> (JOHN 12:46)

Walking in the light sends guilt skulking off into the darkness. Allowing God to shine His light into the hidden recesses of your life takes courage, honesty and self-evaluation. Once you see what He reveals to you, it is your responsibility to yield to the healing and restorative love He offers and make the changes to get you living the life He designed for you. At times the greatest despair of your soul is in knowing what really lurks deep within and yet being afraid to confront it. Jesus is the answer to all the toxic waste in your soul that in turn poisons your relationships. The build-up of waste occurs when there is no outlet. Jesus has provided that way, He is the Outlet and He is more willing to have you guilt-free than you are willing to be free! Internal peace and soundness of mind come when we learn to accept God's gift of guilt-free living. Living with freedom from guilt is obtained and maintained as you are faithful to share your life with God, learn His Word, the Bible, and align your life with His principles and instructions. If God says it, He means it! He promised an abundant life – and that means you can live guilt-free! We take into the world what we know of God. To the depths that we know Him, we make Him known. It is

Exhale guilt and inhale His forgiveness!

29

one thing saying you know God and that you live for Him. It is another thing for people to experience God in you and your life as a shining reflection of Him.

God's heart always has been and always will be for relationships. This is evident from Genesis to Revelation. The first and foremost reason that God created Adam was to have fellowship with Him. To have fellowship means:

- Sharing

- Unity

- Close association

- Participation

- Partnership

Can you imagine the God of all creation desiring to be in personal, unbroken, ever-increasing relationship with you? For all the times you have longed to hear beautiful words in your earthly relationship, God whispers these to you a thousand times more through His Love Letter to you, the Bible. For the times you have longed for acceptance, to be just you, He accepts you unconditionally, for He created you for His good pleasure. Your worth to God was established when He thought about you and then created you. Your worth to Him is not dependent on your material possessions, who your parents are or how successful your career is, or even if your works for charity outnumber the stars. No. God loves you because you are His. God wants you to experience the true riches that come from abiding in His Presence – just as you are, and guilt-free. His Presence equips you to impart His love, joy and peace into the relationships

For all the times you have longed to hear beautiful words in your earthly relationship, God whispers these to you a thousand times more through His Love Letter to you, the Bible.

30

that affect your life. This is true influence. The lives of others begin to change because of the transformation effect you have on their lives. This is being a witness for Christ. Being a witness is just that. The Bible does not say a word about 'doing' a witness for Jesus. Being is knowing; resting, and influencing. Being is the very nature, the very essence of Christ in you, your hope of Glory. Being in His Presence allows you to progressively know Him more intimately. We all need to individually forge our own personal relationship with God. It is not for us to impose this relationship on anyone else, for this relationship cannot be transferred or given away, it is something that each one needs to cultivate personally. In the same way that no one else can build your relationship with your husband for you, neither can another develop your relationship with God. Sound and fulfilling spiritual and natural relationships are built by spending time in each other's presence. It is based on honouring one another to make enough time for each other. God always has the time to meet with you – just ask Him, you'll see.

My Reflections on Living Guilt-Free

❖ Are you truly living the abundant life God intends for you to live? Exhale guilt and inhale His forgiveness!

❖ What do you need to speak to God about today, to get your life on His pathway of joy, peace, success and prosperity?

Be Inspirational – Sensational ❦

Do you live with great expectation and high levels of possibility thinking; ready to go out there and make your mark in the world?

Have you given yourself some well-deserved time to reflect over the past year of your life? Have you taken note to learn from past mistakes to be sure not to repeat them, and have you made the decision to suck the marrow out of the years to come? It is vital that you end each year in victory, in spite of the challenges you may have faced, so that you can close the doors on those things that don't add value or bring joy to your life, and enter the next year with heartfelt inspiration. Overhanging and unresolved matters from previous experiences will keep you perplexed and tired – and not inspired. Whatever is unresolved is sure to leave the door open for you to attract more of the same, and those circumstances will tag along with you into your future. You have to leave a situation in victory in order to enter the next phase of your life in victory. If you leave a situation in defeat, you enter the next situation with a defeatist mindset.

Taking responsibility for your life is the key for building your life of inspiration.

It may be that good relationships seem few and far between, business is becoming more demanding, and indeed the world is not becoming an easier place to live in, with technology seemingly spinning us out of control on one hand, but offering us a whole new world on the other; ethics and integrity are fast becoming non-existent, which makes good business practice even more difficult; not to mention hurricanes, earthquakes and other natural disasters that are assailing our planet. How do we stand tall in this falling world?

But still, all of that is external. Those are things we cannot control. But thankfully, the things we can control and take responsibility for are ourselves, our choices and our attitudes to life.

Taking responsibility for your life is the key for building your life of inspiration. It is amongst the most mature choices of mankind. The Inspired Person is a rare breed; they are in a class of their own. Inspired people have learnt the hard but valuable lesson that life doesn't always go the way they would like it to, but they make the most of it anyway. Take your tragedies and turn them into triumphs. Be an inspiration to others; be that person whose life and ways cause others to look at their own life and realize how much they have to be thankful for. Use the seasons of your life to work for you and don't allow them to work against you. Work harder on yourself than you do on trying to change others. Work harder on yourself than you do on your career. The results will speak for themselves.

'The Inspired Person is confident, but is void of arrogance. Humility is a trademark of the Inspired Person, but they are not doormats. Sensitivity to others is part of who they are, but they are not weak. They are assertive people, but aggression is far from them.'

Ucibus

The Inspired Person knows they were born for a purpose and not by accident. Know that you have been created to live an abundant life and not a redundant life. Welcome and embrace your uniqueness and forget about wasting your time on comparing yourself with others, or trying to be like them. At the same time, know the value of having a role model, but keep your individuality and uniqueness.

The Inspired Person knows they are created by God and they are able to inspire others to greatness. They live their lives being focused on becoming everything they were created to be and are done with frittering away their lives on the immaterial and non-essentials.

Life is not so much about what happens to us, but rather, what we do with what happens to us. The truth is the challenges of life come to us all; rich or poor, married or single, educated or uneducated. The real attribute that sets the Inspired Person apart is that they make sound choices to be sure they don't attract negative, abusive, and destructive situations into their lives.

Being inspirational is fundamentally all about the attitude you choose to have about life. Life offers no guarantees. We don't know why bad things happen to good people, but we do have a choice about how we respond to these things. Now is the time to stop wrestling with the things you cannot change or don't understand, and make the most of what you have and change what you can change. We generally make a change for one of two reasons: either we are inspired to change, or we are desperate for change. Either way, make the change today! You are not limited to the way you are living now unless you choose it to be so.

The truth is this: you have resident within you one of the most powerful gifts God has given to you. It is the gift that no one should be able to touch or take from you. It is the one thing that designs your life moment by moment. This is your gift of choice.

What is CHOICE…?

Choosing
How
Our
Individual
Circumstances
Evolve

Our choices determine our destiny.
What we choose today, we will live through tomorrow.

My Reflections on Being
Inspirational and Sensational

✧   Choose today, this year and the rest of your life to be inspirational and sensational!

✧   How?

The Seed of Greatness is Within You

'YOUR BEGINNINGS WILL SEEM HUMBLE, SO PROSPEROUS WILL YOUR FUTURE BE!'
(JOB 8:7)

The seed. The beginning of greatness. To get where you want to be, you need to start with what you have. If you have faith even as small as a mustard seed – the smallest of all the seeds – nothing shall be impossible for you. In Jesus' own words:

> *'I tell you the truth, if you have faith as small as a mustard seed, you can say to this mountain, 'Move from here to there' and it will move. Nothing will be impossible for you.'*
> (MATTHEW 17:20)

Every seed that you sow will produce after its own kind. You will produce after your own kind. If you want to know what kind of a leader you are, look at your followers – your family, your staff and your friends. What are they saying, what are they doing? It is quite likely that they have taken a leaf out of your book. Every day of your life you are planting seeds that will give you a harvest in one form or another. Life truly is about sowing and reaping. The harvest is not instant. Sometimes it takes years to come forth, but it will surely make itself known. Never underestimate the power of your associations and decisions in life to take you up or to drop you low.

Hidden inside you lie seeds of significance and greatness. Ensure that you keep planting your seeds in the soil of this truth. Plant your seeds in areas where you want them to grow. Both poverty and riches are seeds that have been planted in your belief system. Success or failure is the harvest of seed sown. Seeds of doubt and procrastination bear fruit of delay and frustration. Seeds of persistence and determination reward you with great results.

Your life will follow your expectation.

Success or failure is not one big cataclysmic event, but rather a series of choices you have made over a period of time. Every opportunity you are waiting for will come as a response to the seed you have sown.

What you conceive and believe, God and you can most certainly achieve.

Imagination is a seed that must be planted in order to bring forth the desires that stir in your heart. You must conceive an idea in your heart and mind before you can achieve it. That is the law of sowing and reaping. Unless you are willing to plant good seed, you will not reap a great harvest. What you keep in mind will produce after its own kind. Your life will follow your expectation. You have to change your thinking before you can ever change your way of living. Choose to live in the seed – the attitude that great things are going to happen every day for you. What can you lose by having great expectations? You will lose bad expectations! What a great trade.

You first have to conceive an idea in your imagination, and then believe it before you can receive it. This is the seed planting process. Your mind has to be fertile; ready to receive the seed so you can plant the imagination – the desire, which to your mind may seem impossible at present. This is faith in action. Planting seeds of faith is going to give you a harvest of success. Planting seeds of doubt will bring failure. Don't sabotage your crop by planting the seeds of questioning, reasoning and doubt. Plant in faith! To achieve what you want to achieve you have to plant the right seed. Don't allow mediocrity to become your norm. Don't let past successes become your ceiling. Mentally rehearse the greater victories. There is no human power that can put a stop to unity, determination and creative imagination. Only God can! The book of Genesis, Chapter 11 speaks of the whole earth being of one language and mode of expression. The people of the day agreed to build a city and a tower whose top reached into the sky, so that they could make a name for themselves. (Once again man wanted to usurp the place of God!) The Lord came down to see the city and the tower that the sons of men had built. And the Lord said, *'Behold, they are one people and they have all one language; and this is only the beginning of what they will do, and now nothing they have IMAGINED they can do will be IMPOSSIBLE for them.'* Such is the power that God has released in our ability to imagine. Nothing will be impossible. Many of the inventions in the world today prove this. One push of a red button and a nation can be turned into vapour! Let us always be sure that those things that we are birthing in our imagination are aligned with God's purposes and are not at cross-purposes with God, otherwise we too might have our language and our lives confounded! The power of construction and destruction lies in the imagination.

> *'We are told never to cross a bridge till we come to it, but the world is owned by men and women who have crossed bridges in their imagination far ahead of the crowd.'*
> JOHN L. MASON

When you plant a seed of the impossible with God, you invite purpose, passion and determination to be activated in your life. Passion gives you energy and the will to fulfil that purpose. Passion gives you the adrenaline to push through even when everyone else is telling you it can't be done. People who live without passion are usually people without a dream. Passion for the seemingly impossible should excite, ignite and delight you! Why stay stuck in the rut of routine when God has blessed you with His ability to dream, to imagine, to create something out of nothing. Everything in this world was once somebody's idea! He who sees the invisible can achieve the impossible.

You see things; and you say, 'Why?' But I dream things that never were; and I say, 'Why not?'
GEORGE BERNARD SHAW

So what are you passionate about?

- What dream drives your life?

- What has heart and meaning for your life?

- What is it that you so desperately want to do, but keep putting off?

- What on earth are you waiting for?

- What has to happen before you will allow yourself the freedom to dream?

Martin Luther King was a man with a God-given talent. He had a dream. In his well-renowned speech, he did not say:

'I have a wish, or a feeling…'

But rather he powerfully declared, 'I have a dream that one day…' And that day came – and changed the world forever!

You will be amazed at the doors of opportunity waiting to open up to you. You will stand in awe at how many people are waiting for your dream to come their way. You will be astonished at what you can achieve when you believe in your seed of greatness that has been deposited in you by God. You are made in the image of God – how can there not be greatness within you?

Be open to a lifetime of possibilities!

Your sense of purpose must be one of the major pillars of your life. Your purpose is what makes you get out of bed in the morning with hope for the day ahead. Purpose gives you direction in the routine of daily tasks. Purpose means living your life with intent and determination. To live without a reason, without purpose, means you live with no hope – only tasks that need to be done. To live with no hope means that you have no dream for your future. God is the Author of purpose, and dreams – be sure to be plugged into the spout where the Power comes out! Greatness comes to the one who has the ability to take life with all its twists and turns and make the very best of it, learning and applying the lessons to their life, all the way. There is a world of opportunity on the inside of you. Give the world the gift of your life.

The purpose of life is to live a life of purpose.

ROBERT BYRNE

Find a need and fill it and you will never be out of business. Today is the first day of the very best days of your life. Be done with mediocrity and live your one magnificent life for God.

Relationally knowing Jesus Christ gives you understanding of your reason for being. Knowing His purpose for your life will establish your uniqueness and distinctiveness in Him; the One Who embodies purpose. He will forever answer your questions of 'Who am I and what is the meaning of my life?' He addresses your importance and your purpose in this life, always.

If you are still here, God isn't through with you yet!

My Reflections on the Seeds of Greatness that Lie Within Me

✧ When last did you truly reflect on your life and its meaning?

✧ What does your harvest look like currently? Is it time to sow some different seeds?

Free to Choose ✒

'SHOW ME YOUR WAYS, O LORD; TEACH ME YOUR PATHS. GUIDE ME IN YOUR TRUTH
AND FAITHFULNESS AND TEACH ME, FOR YOU ARE THE GOD OF MY SALVATION; FOR YOU
DO I WAIT ALL THE DAY LONG.'
(PSALM 25:4,5A)

To choose is to decide your destiny. To compromise your freedom to choose is the first step towards your defeat. Of all the manifold blessings God has given you, one of the most powerful gifts you have been endowed with is the ability to choose. You have been given the gift of choice. Your choices today determine your tomorrow. Your life is the outworking of your daily, compounded choices. The outcome of your life is determined by whose instructions you follow. To choose is to exercise your free will. You win or you lose by the way you choose. God will never violate your freedom to choose. If He did, you would be a robot and therefore could not be expected to be accountable for how you have conducted this one life He has given you. You are in the privileged position of being able to choose in every given circumstance. There may have been many times that others have succeeded in violating your free will, but the one power they can never have is how you choose to respond to the violation. Every choice from the smallest to the most major of your life's decisions will have an outcome. The results often last a lifetime.

You win or you lose by the way that you choose!

One of the greatest gifts you can give back to God is your free will. When you align your will to His ways, you are assured that you will be on the right track to start making right choices. The general consensus today is that, 'This is my life and I can spend it anyway I choose. You can't make me do anything I don't want to do. I have a free will and I will use it how I want.' All of that is true. Your will is free, but it is one of the most expensive possessions you own. Exercising your free will negatively in the moment can mean a lifetime of regret and consequence. Just ask a pregnant teenager, or a husband faced with divorce because of a momentary interlude with someone who does not even feature in his life. What about a random act of anger that means a lifelong prison sentence? Similarly, exercising your free will in making good, Godly choices every day will bring a harvest of abundant life. Choice lets you know how powerful it is when you begin to reap what you have sown. God, by giving man a free will has, by His choice, placed limits on His own power, i.e. He will not override your free will.

> *Promise me you'll always remember: you're braver than you believe, and stronger than you seem, and smarter than you think.*
>
> WINNIE THE POOH

Amongst the pivotal lessons I have learned on this journey of life is that my choices, always without exception, have a source. Without exception that source is my thought processes. We think tens of thousands of thoughts every day. It is an alarming fact that every single one of those thoughts will find a way of expression. Each thought is a seed planted in the fertile soil of your heart, it takes root and when it is fully grown it will bear fruit! You can always judge the root of an issue by the fruit it bears. A good root cannot produce bad fruit and a bad root cannot produce good fruit! Fruit always produces after its own kind.

> *Never underestimate the power of what you believe even if it is only a perception.*
>
> STEPHEN COVEY

Your entire being is impacted by the thoughts you hold. Your thoughts about God, about yourself and about others will always lead you to act out what you believe. Your thoughts and perceptions are the springboard for your reactions. Your thoughts determine your feelings. They form your attitudes that determine your behaviour and then thoughts manifest in the spoken, creative word. Mark Twain once said, *'I have known a great many troubles, but most of them never happened.'* Most of them only took place in his mind – but they were very real nonetheless! Once you begin to corkscrew in your thought processes, it is not long before you have vivid pictures in your mind, the full impact of your emotions racing around within and, all too soon, you are reacting to something that is not even a reality. This can work in your favour if your thought processes are edifying but they will work against you if your thoughts have their root in fear, suspicion or unbelief. Every single thought you have is contributing one way or another to the overall result of your one life.

Stephen Covey quotes, *'Never underestimate the power of what you believe, even if it is only a perception.'* In other words, what you think you believe you will believe. Your perceptions become your reality. Your thoughts and feelings are your responsibility. It is important that you recognize your thoughts as they arise, and it is just as crucial for you to *What is revealed* recognize your feelings as they surface. Feelings *can be healed!* left unchecked can overwhelm you, particularly if they are not referred back to your thoughts, the source of your feelings. Introspection is healthy and necessary and you are exhorted in the Word of God to examine yourself:

> *'For if we would judge ourselves, we would not be judged.'*
> (1 CORINTHIANS 11:31)

It is often because of the frantic pace of life that you do not stop to take the time to examine your thoughts and feelings and find yourself living through relentless, often life-destructive patterns. David prayed and asked God thus:

> *'Cleanse me from secret faults. Keep back your servant from*
> *presumptuous sins; let them not have dominion over me. Then I*
> *shall be blameless, and I shall be innocent of great transgression.*
> *Let the words of my mouth and the meditation of my heart be*
> *acceptable in Your sight, O Lord, my strength and my Redeemer.'*
> (PSALM 19:13,14)

Any feeling, symptom or manifestation of behaviour recognized for what it is, is usually the first step towards overcoming it. A doctor cannot prescribe the correct medication until the diagnosis as to the cause is established. It is the same for you. You cannot take corrective action until the root of the problem has been revealed. What is revealed can be healed. It takes choosing openness, honesty and transparency with God and yourself. The Truth revealed in God's Word and diligently applied to your life will set you free. When your unchecked thoughts rule you, you live with uneasy, uncomfortable feelings that express themselves in words. Harmful words can be numbered along with other destructive forces on the earth. Words allowed to spew forth out of your wrangled emotions can create damage to others and often lead to a loss of closeness and intimacy and, sometimes, even the loss of relationships.

Your foot can slip and you can retrieve it, but when your words are out, there is no getting them back. The way they return is by delivering back to you what you have spoken in anger or judgement.

> 'Death and life are in the power of the tongue,
> and those who love it will eat its fruit.'
> (PROVERBS 18:21)

You are free to choose the words you use!

Standing tall in a falling world is going to be determined by the thoughts you have and the words you speak.

My Reflections on My Freedom to Choose

Wishing is Not a Strategy ✍

'ARISE FROM THE DEPRESSION AND PROSTRATION IN WHICH CIRCUMSTANCES HAVE KEPT YOU – RISE TO A NEW LIFE! SHINE (BE RADIANT WITH THE GLORY OF THE LORD), FOR YOUR LIGHT HAS COME, AND THE GLORY OF THE LORD AS RISEN UPON YOU!'
(ISAIAH 60:1, AMP)

It is time to arise, to shine and to rule and reign over the affairs of your life with the help of the Lord. Now is the time to stand tall in this falling world. It is time to leave your wish lists behind and step out into faith-filled action. It is time to bring your influence and intuition to your world and to leave your indifference behind. It is indeed for a time such as this that you have been made ready. Never again will you have the opportunity to live your one magnificent life, even in the midst of mediocrity beckoning you to follow its seemingly easier route. In the process of meandering and moving through life, do you forget to stop and realize the magnificence of your one life? Many people I meet remark on the fact that they want to start living a wonderful life and that they would love to experience the abundant life that Jesus came to give. My response is to ask them what on earth or in heaven are they waiting for? What has to happen before you start to arise and be everything you were created to be in spirit, in soul and in body?

> *What are you waiting for? Do away with your wish lists and step out into faith-filled action.*

We spend way too many of our years wishing our life away…

I wish I could lose weight. I wish I was healthier.
I wish I was happier in my life. I wish I had a husband.
I wish I didn't have a husband. I wish I had more money.
I wish I had a different boss. I wish I could be successful.
I wish I had someone else's opportunities.

On and on you go, wishing your life away but never doing anything concrete about creating the strategy to reach your desires. Your days get washed away as you wait for the circumstances in your life to change, when in actual fact everything you need to be successful is already on the inside of you. You could well be feeling fatigued, bored, sick or tired even as you read this book. You have worn yourself out and are feeling wasted from going around the same rugged mountain for far too long. You are tired from travelling on that weary old road of keeping stale associations with people who add no value to your life, of doing the same boring routines day in and day out, wishing things could be different and promising yourself that tomorrow they will! Wishing is not a strategy. Putting action to your desires is!

The will must be stronger than the skill.

MUHAMMAD ALI

You can spend years trying to rearrange the external things, but until you arrest your thoughts, shift your stuck mindset, and realign your focus, change will not be lasting or satisfying. I can already hear your protests that I don't understand your circumstances or your load. All of us have our overloaded trailers that we need to dump off at some stage of our lives. I may not understand your circumstances, but I do know for sure that you never have to be a victim of your past, your present or your perceived future, and that your strategy for life can change from wishful to wonderful. All that remains is to ask yourself how you can build the bridge by making the right choices and by doing things more effectively and purposefully that will take you from wishing to wonderful experience, and from mediocrity to magnificence in your approach to life.

Celebrate instead of abdicate!

Challenges come to every human being. It is not so much what happens to you that counts, but how you respond to what happens to you that really matters. One of the features of a mature person is that they have learned to respond to a situation instead of reacting. Someone

49

once said that 10% of life is what happens to you, and 90% of life is how you respond to what happens to you. You have to live through the 90% for longer than the 10% impact. This is where you really see how empowered and determined you are. Reactive people are restricted people. Once they have reacted there is no freedom to respond. Most often their guilt causes them to be even more restricted and their next reaction is worse than the first, and so a vicious cycle of victim behaviour, often accompanied by aggression, ensues. Reactive behaviour rapes your freedom to choose. You win or you lose by the way that you choose. A reactive mentality creates a victim mentality and victims don't live very happy lives. Being a victim makes one feel helpless and hopeless and often that is the starting point of wishing, which then becomes your negative strategy for life. Hopelessness is totally disempowering. You can choose today to live your life by design or by default. Reverting to behaviour by default requires no forethought. Someone just needs to push your sensitive or unresolved 'button' and you react – boom – just like that! Some behaviour is so deeply entrenched that the person reacting does not even realize they have reacted, until it is too late. It has simply become a way of life for them. This is default behaviour, and default behaviour is potentially life-threatening in that it can affect your relationships, and your health, due to the stress and tension created by anger and uncontrolled emotional outbursts. Living by default means that you remain stuck in the same patterns and destructive cycles that keep you entrapped and victimized.

Reactive people are restricted people.

Standing tall when your world is falling requires that you choose to colour your world by turning your wish list into strategy, as opposed to living your life in dismal black and white. You may wish for a different job, you may desire to move house or even to another country, but you will take yourself with you wherever you go. You are going to change, either because you are driven by desperation, or inspired by transformation. Whichever one it is, I trust you will begin to make the changes that will work for you and not against you. You cannot change anyone else but you certainly can make changes within yourself that will enable you to bring focus, stability and strategy to your world. Why have such a low expectation of yourself when, in fact, you can achieve so much by being prepared to put action to your life and stop wishing your life away? Step out of that depression, climb out of those circumstances and arise and shine, for your light has come! Change is one choice away. Strategy is about having a plan, a specific approach, a tactic that can make your life fantastic. You choose.

'You have brains in your head.
You have feet in your shoes.
You can steer yourself any direction you choose.'

Dr Seuss, *Oh, the Places You'll Go!*

My Reflections on Believing in Place of Wishing; Putting Strategy to My Wishes

✧ Today I say goodbye to my black-and-white world of rut, routine and wishful thinking.

✧ I stand tall as I face the challenges that are designed for my growth and strengthening. Breakthrough becomes my strategy!

✧ What shifts do I need to make in my thinking, in my approach and in my planning to walk in the life I was designed to live?

....

....

....

....

....

....

....

....

....

....

....

....

....

....

....

....

....

Chapter Two

~

Standing Tall in Your Body

Body – your body is your ever-present companion. Nurture it and it will nurture you. Look after it and it will reward you. For no matter how awesome your dream for your life may be, if your body is in a state of disrepair, achieving that dream will take far more effort, energy and commitment than if your body is fully alive and well. Your body is what houses your spirit and your soul. Your body is that part of you that everyone sees, but it is not necessarily the 'real' you. People spend excessive amounts on presenting the outside of themselves to the world, but sadly oftentimes spend far too little time and attention working on the inside, which is where the 'real' person is formed.

Your body is your 'earthly vehicle' and it requires quality nutrition and water to function at optimal capacity. It further requires to be exercised and to be in motion and movement very frequently. Unfortunately in today's environment our bodies are seizing up because of a lack of movement, they are dying young because of the high levels of stress under which people live and they are being poisoned because of the lifestyle habits that slowly destroy immune systems and energy levels, and negatively impact a general sense of wellbeing.

It is time to embrace your body. Treat it as if it is going to last you a lifetime. Cut out the destructive habits, get enough sleep, drink more water, eliminate debilitating stress factors and really start living today!

Be Alive All the Days of Your Life 🌿

YOU ARE FEARFULLY AND WONDERFULLY MADE!

'*For you formed my inward parts; You covered me in my mother's womb. I will praise You, for I am fearfully and wonderfully made; Marvellous are Your works, and that my soul knows very well. My frame was not hidden from You when I was made in secret, and skilfully wrought in the lowest parts of the earth. Your eyes saw my substance, being yet unformed. And in Your book they were all written, the days fashioned for me, when as yet there were none of them. How precious also are Your thoughts to me, O God! How great is the sum of them! If I should count them, they would be more in number than the sand; when I awake I am still with You.' (Psalm 139:13–18)*

We have all been apportioned a time to live and a time to die. The time in between is our responsibility to do everything we possibly can to keep our lives reflective of the life of Christ within. Jesus came to give us life full of joy unspeakable and full of glory. Man-made religion has made life rigid with rules and regulations, denying the power and freedom of a life in Christ. You and I can only be alive all the days of our lives when we take ownership of the fact that the most satisfying life we can live is when we live God's way.

> '*When a man's ways please the Lord, He makes*
> *even his enemies to be at peace with him. A man's*
> *heart plans his way, but the Lord directs his steps.*
> *Understanding is a wellspring of life to him who has it.*'
> (PROVERBS 16:7, 9,22)

Your body is the Temple of the Holy Spirit and you owe it to God and to yourself to give it the respect and care that it deserves. There are many negative opportunities in this falling world to destroy you – spirit, soul and body. To stand tall takes continual determined decisions and a strong will that defies the temptations to overeat, to drink irresponsibly, to give in to laziness and shun exercise, and become trapped by the tentacles of mindless television and feed on the negativity of communications that can entrench fear, depression and debilitating thinking into your life.

Paul writing to the Roman Church in AD56 has some very sound advice for us alive on the earth today:

> 'So here's what I want you to do, God helping you: Take
> your everyday, ordinary life – your sleeping, eating, going-
> to-work, and walking-around life – and place it before God
> as an offering. Embracing what God does for you is the best
> thing you can do for Him. Don't become so well adjusted
> to your culture that you fit into it without even thinking.
> Instead, fix your attention on God. You'll be changed from the
> inside out. Readily recognize what He wants from you, and
> quickly respond to it. Unlike the culture around you, always
> dragging you down to its level of immaturity, God brings the
> best out of you, develops well-formed maturity in you.'
> (ROMANS 12:1–2)

There are many voices in society each with a different opinion on about a million topics. How are you ever to know what is true and for you? I personally have adopted the words of life that are found in the Bible as the personal authority for my life. The Word of God is eternal and unchanging and with Him I know there is no shadow of turning, He can be trusted and His word is a gift, His promise for life.

> 'Every good and perfect gift is from above, and
> comes down from the Father of lights, with whom
> there is no variation or shadow of turning.'
> (JAMES 1:17)

The guidance found in His Word is true and sound and, when applied by you with faith, enhances your life and allows you to be alive all the days of your life.

*'All Scripture is given by inspiration of God, and is
profitable for doctrine, for reproof, for correction, for
instruction in righteousness that the man of God may be
complete, thoroughly equipped for every good work.'*
(2 TIMOTHY 3:16,17)

You cannot escape the responsibility of tomorrow by evading it today.

ABRAHAM LINCOLN,
16TH PRESIDENT OF THE USA

What I love about God's personal attention towards us is that He is intricately involved with matters of our health, what we feed our minds on, how well we eat and take care of our bodies and our personal hygiene; not to mention how to live in the present and for eternity. The Bible is the most practical day-to-day handbook that empowers and offers great rewards for right living. The decisions you make today about your daily habits and your lifestyle will be experienced in your life tomorrow, and the next day, and your next life.

So how do you conduct your day-to-day life?

Keeping a light heart through the heavy challenges of your day is paramount.

*'A merry heart does good like medicine, but
a broken spirit dries the bones.'*
(PROVERBS 17:22)

Being cheerful keeps you young in heart and face, and in great health. Keep a good, clean sense of humour; it's a great companion while travelling along the road of your life. Pass through this world travelling light. Dump the baggage and do not be loaded down with anything more than you have to. Anger is a heavy and dangerous burden and there is no way you can walk free and be alive while anger has dominion in your life.

*'Do not hasten in your spirit to be angry, for
anger rests in the bosom of fools.'*
(ECCLESIASTES 7:9)

Could this be why so many people are suffering with breast cancer? Negative emotions never just go away; they express themselves in other areas of your life. Being depressed, anxious, wrought-up and negative will also weigh you down and suck the life out of you.

> *'Be anxious for nothing, but in everything by*
> *prayer and supplication, with thanksgiving, let*
> *your requests be made known to God.'*
> (PHILIPPIANS 4:6)

Thanksgiving opens a doorway for freedom, joy and great blessing.

There are many reasons for displaying negative emotions and having them rule your life. Much of this has been addressed in other chapters of this book; however, the very practical matters of life can also be a source of your feeling blue.

> *'Remember happiness doesn't depend upon who you are or*
> *what you have; it depends solely upon what you think. So start*
> *each day thinking of all the things you have to be thankful for. Your*
> *future will depend very largely on the thoughts you think today. So*
> *think thoughts of hope and confidence and love and success.'*
> DALE CARNEGIE, LEADERSHIP TRAINING FOR MANAGERS
> JOHANNESBURG, SOUTH AFRICA, 1994

One thing every human being does each day is eat. What we eat probably negatively affects us in more ways than we would care to stop and think about. Since our lives are hectic and often eating is done on the run, time is not taken to think about what we are putting in our bodies. To oversimplify the point, eating what is natural is best. When you are selecting off a menu, try to choose that which is protein and vegetable ahead of starch or synthetics. Avoid overeating – it makes you fat!

Drinking water is drinking life! You simply cannot function to your optimal potential when your body and brain are dehydrated. Drink as much water as you possibly can each day and don't substitute that water with anything else. That is not to say coffee, tea and fruit juice are banned, but just don't let them become a substitute for water. Our body is made up of 70% water – I guess it is a no-brainer as to the reasons why we should drink more than a litre of water each day!

> *'Oh listen dear child – become wise; point your life in the*
> *right direction. Don't drink too much wine and get drunk;*
> *don't eat too much food and get fat. Drunks and gluttons*
> *will end up on skid row, in a stupor and dressed in rags.'*
> (PROVERBS 23:21)

Get regular exercise. It is really one of the ways you can add such enormous value to your life. In our modern lifestyles, we drive cars, sit in office chairs and stare at a computer screen, and the only things that get exercise are our fingers as they move around the keypad. Movement is life and we need to keep our bodies moving. There is much research and evidence available in support of weight-bearing and resistance exercises to give muscle tone, build strength and to avoid osteoporosis. Energy levels are raised and a general feel-good sense of life comes back to you when you make the decision to exercise with commitment three or more times per week. The older you get the more your body needs exercise to strengthen your back and your bones. Don't delay, start today!

Sleep is the bed of life! You cannot possibly hope to function at optimal capacity if you are tired and irritable from lack of sleep. Sleep deprivation is used as a torture method for a reason you know! You cannot give what you do not have and so much of your life is restored to you as you sleep restfully and peacefully.

> *'But you, God, shield me on all sides; You ground my feet,*
> *you lift my head high; with all my might I shout up to God, His*
> *answers thunder from the holy mountain. I stretch myself out.*
> *I sleep. Then I'm up again – rested, tall and steady, fearless*
> *before the enemy mobs coming at me from all sides.'*
> (PSALM 3:3–7)

Everything you do from day to day in your one life is another entry in your Book of Life. You are creating a legacy that one day will be read by those coming after you. Each day you are painting another stroke on the canvas of your life. What self-portrait are you leaving?

> 'Seize life! Eat bread with gusto, drink wine with a robust heart. Oh yes – God takes pleasure in your pleasure! Dress festively every morning. Don't skimp on colours and scarves. Relish life with the spouse you love each and every day of your precarious life. Each day is God's gift. It's all you get in exchange for the hard work of staying alive. Make the most of each one! Whatever turns up, grab it and do it. And heartily!'
>
> (ECCLESIASTES 9:7–9)

Desire is the ingredient that changes the hot water of mediocrity to the steam of outstanding success.

ZIG ZIGLAR

My Reflections on Being Alive!

✧ Take some time to analyse what you eat and how you can bring exercise into your daily life.

✧ Why live limply at half-mast when you can be flying high and be alive all the days of your life?

Movement is Life ✌

'ANYONE WHO STOPS LEARNING IS OLD, WHETHER AT TWENTY OR EIGHTY. ANYONE WHO KEEPS LEARNING STAYS YOUNG. THE GREATEST THING IN LIFE IS TO KEEP YOUR MIND YOUNG.'
HENRY FORD

Ageing and stagnation are not about your age. They are more about the lack of movement in your body, your mind and in your daily life. Stiff and unused muscles can become arthritic when you limit your movement. Where there is no movement there is no fluidity. Everything feels like it is drying up. The ultimate lack of movement is death. I am always interested in a person who is in their 70s or 80s and who has extraordinary amounts of energy and life in them. Examine them closely enough and the reason becomes clear. They have not resorted to inactivity, either mentally or physically. When you stop moving you start dying.

Do not squander time for it is the stuff that life is made of.
BENJAMIN FRANKLIN

It is fascinating to notice how God's instructions are mostly around the word: Go! Even more interesting is that these two letters are the first two letters of God's Name. From the beginning of the Bible to its close, there are instructions such as: *'arise, get up, take your mat, move on, take the land, press forward, go forth!'* Life is meant to be lived; you were designed to be fruitful and productive and to multiply that which you do. Stagnation is the absence of productivity. There is a great difference between being busy and being productive. Ensure that those things in which you invest so much of your precious time and energy are going to multiply and give you a return.

*'It is a mistake to regard age as a downhill grade
toward dissolution. The reverse is true. As one grows
older one climbs with surprising strides.'*
GEORGE SAND

61

> *Life is a progress and not a station.*
>
> <small>RALPH WALDO EMERSON</small>

Being at peace and at a place of rest within yourself does not equate to doing nothing. You can be wildly productive but still be in total peace. Being in a place of confident rest and peace in the Lord is an act of faith – it is really a rest in your inner man – a peacefulness; stillness – while the outer man is taking action. It is like marching on the spot or treading water.

Very often when you sense a lack of fulfilment in God, it is because you have slowed down or have stopped and have lost connection with God. He keeps moving. Fulfilment in God is at its best when you stay connected and keep in step with Him; this is the place where there is no separation between you and God. When He says go, you go. When He says speak, you speak. When He says, have faith, abide in me… then you abide. Being at peace with God in your heart is the opposite of living from a heart full of fear, panic, hopelessness and despair. Living, moving and having your being centred in God is living in continual Divine Connection and in a Heaven-on-Earth relationship.

> *All glory comes from daring to begin.*
>
> <small>EUGENE F. WARE</small>

Standing tall in a falling world requires living from a place of real closeness with the Lord. It is experiencing what the Bible talks about when Adam knew Eve. It is a Hebrew word called 'Yada', which means intimacy as a husband knows his wife. In other words, because you are so intimate in living your life with God, you know and acknowledge His thoughts towards you, you know His quietest whisper, and you know when He is telling you to move on. Perhaps He is telling you that right now? So often I have had people telling me that they are waiting; waiting for this to happen, or for a sign or confirmation of something they should be doing. In the meantime they have become discouraged, they lack vitality and have lost energy. Quite honestly, some are lifeless. Rather do something productive and work towards that which you desire, than be idle and lose steam. Don't confuse waiting with idleness. Waiting should not be wasting.

It is time to make the shift, to move forward, to move on from your past, from your place of shame, from your seat of inactivity! Movement is doing the right things daily that will give you results even if you don't see them immediately. You can keep moving in faith, in hope and with confidence because of Jesus.

'Now faith is being sure of what we hope
for and certain of what we do not see.'
(HEBREWS 11:1)

He can redeem every area of need or lack in your life. Grab a hold of this truth and stagnate no more. Remove the repeat offenders in your life – those things that keep you entrapped need to exit your life today. Do whatever it takes to get your momentum back. Break out of your entrenched mindset that keeps you in limitation and in lack. Move forward to the next phase of your life that God has designed and detailed for you. Moses had to 'stretch forth' before the Red Sea parted. Joshua had to 'march' before the walls of Jericho fell. David had to 'wind up his sling' before he could slay Goliath. Do whatever it takes to 'stretch forth' into the next phase of your life.

> *Within you right now is the power to do things you never dreamed possible. This power becomes available to you just as soon as you can change your beliefs.*
>
> MAXWELL MALTZ

'Enlarge the place of your tent, and let the curtains of
your habitations be stretched out; spare not; lengthen
your cords and strengthen your stakes, for you will
spread abroad to the right hand and to the left...'
(ISAIAH 54:2,3)

Productivity attracts promotion and prosperity. Healing brings wholeness. Dare to dream again. Jump for joy!

Believe, see and experience the favour of God in your life. He is waiting to bless you today as you arise from your slumber. Jump out of your thimble of water and into His vast ocean of purpose and productivity. There is so much that awaits you. Don't settle for so little when He wants to bless you with so much. Swim out to the place that is over your head. This is a new place, an enlarged place; it is new territory you are gaining. Start to decree to the places that must open up before you – 'Here I come!' Whether in your relationships, your finances, in the area of promotion – the favour of God and the invitation of God are upon you when you move forward in faith.

My Reflections on Movement in My Life

✧ What have you got to confront in order to step out into that ocean of blessing?

✧ What are those giants in your land that must be overcome? Fears, laziness, discouragement, people, situations, secret sins, financial debt?

✧ If you could see what God has in store for you, you would never be disabled by a lack of movement and momentum again.

Your Personal Powerful Brand ❧

EMPOWERMENT MEANS THAT YOU DON'T HAVE TO WAIT FOR APPROVAL FROM ANYONE TO POSSESS WHAT GOD HAS GIVEN YOU.

I'm sure you have heard the saying, 'Who you are speaks so loudly, I cannot hear what you are saying!' That is what being, and presenting yourself well, without saying a word, is all about. Your personal grooming, image and overall appearance is your unique personal outward branding. Who you are has your signature all over it. Be confident in your image, don't apologize for who you are. It is your individual uniqueness that makes the world such a colourful place. It is your inner and outer branding that makes your mark on this world.

> *Your life is up to you. Life provides the canvas; you do the painting.*
>
> ANONYMOUS

Go prepared to market yourself before you attempt to promote or sell anything else. Wake up well and present yourself well to your family each day. Be confident as you walk into your place of work each morning, market yourself brilliantly before you try to sell a customer your product, and get yourself a dose of joy before you answer a telephone. Great personal grooming and a confident image go a long way to 'get the ears' of the people you meet, and it helps build a positive expectation. The greater the expectation you build of yourself into someone, the more they will want to know you; and you in turn can respond with even greater levels of confidence, which almost always opens doors for fabulous and profitable opportunities.

For people to be comfortable with you, you must first be comfortable with yourself. Stand up straight, set your shoulders square, hold your head up and look them straight in the eye when you address them. Project confidence even if you don't always feel confident. Remember this; most people always appear more confident than they really are. Be

66

able to laugh at yourself when you make mistakes, or perhaps when you get tongue-tied or lose your train of thought. This makes you seem real and approachable and it often establishes your credibility in the heart and mind of the person with whom you are communicating.

Take the time each day to groom and be the very best *you* you can be. You only have one body, one skin, one heart and one life. Use these precious possessions wisely and make the most of them. Regardless of how serious your ambitions, or how dramatic your dreams, you need a body to get you there. Whilst the human body is a very powerful machine, and is

> *Failure is only the opportunity to begin again more intelligently.*
>
> HENRY FORD

self-healing and resilient, it needs your best care to be the finest serving body it can be. Exercise is of paramount importance in your life. It is often a challenge to find the time to exercise and stretch, but better to find the time now while you have the chance of being toned and fit, rather than being saddled with regret that you didn't start years ago. Even 10–15 minutes a day of moderate exercise can make a difference to the way you feel. Couple this exercise with a great eating plan – no, not a diet – stringent diets definitely don't work in the long term; but a sound, well-balanced eating plan incorporating foods that contain natural nutrients that your body was designed to digest, can make the world of difference to your life. Consuming natural and wholesome foods can positively change your daily life from fatigued to fabulous. We are, after all, what we eat. Make the choice to eat nutri-dense foods such as colourful fruit and vegetables, white meat, fish and other proteins. Cut back on the bland and man-made foods, and there is no limit to how much life-giving water you may drink.

> *There is only one way to succeed in anything, and that is to give everything.*
>
> VINCE LOMBARDI

Your one skin can either be radiant and youthful or puckered and pruned all the years of your life. The choice is yours. Water is life and if your skin has one need, water is surely it. A daily sunscreen is another. Just taking a few extra minutes each day to moisturize and screen your face could be the most wonderful gift you give your face. At night, your skin needs to breathe: cleanse, tone and use a light night cream to nourish and rest your skin. Doing these few small things every day will take years away from your skin's inevitable ageing process. And for your sake, cut out the nicotine! One cigarette devours mega milligrams of Vitamin C, the vital element for creating collagen, which gives your skin the elasticity to make you look youthful. Love the skin you have been given. Care for it and it will treat you well. All the money in the world can't buy you health and vitality, but you can take the time today to start doing the all-important things to give yourself the best opportunities to live the kind of life you desire and to live a life you can be proud of. It is time to stand tall – overall!

Knowledge alone is not power; it needs to be properly applied for it to be truly powerful.

One decision is all it takes to get a different result in your life. You may be feeling as though you have tried 20 different diets and have started an exercise programme 100 times over but you have never followed through with it. The question you have to answer is, 'How much do I want this new look/a healthy lifestyle/beautiful skin/or cleaner lungs?' The degree to which you really want the above, is the degree to which you will commit to making changes to your daily lifestyle. Pray and ask God to empower your choices and your ability to stick with the programme. He is all for us living the abundant life. He has given us a future and hope, but let us be sure we do our part to capitalize on the fullness of that abundance.

'You've all been to the stadium and seen the athletes' race. Everyone runs; one wins. Run to win. All good athletes train hard. They do it for a gold medal that tarnishes and fades. You're after one that's gold eternally. I don't know about you,

*but I'm running hard for the finish line. I'm giving it everything
I've got. No sloppy living for me! I'm staying alert and in
top condition. I'm not going to get caught napping, telling
everyone else all about it and then missing out myself.'*

(THE WORDS OF PAUL, THE APOSTLE – 1 CORINTHIANS 9:24–27)

My Reflections on My Personal Powerful Brand

'Happiness is when what you think, what you say and what you do are in harmony.'
Mahatma Gandhi

....

....

....

....

....

....

....

....

....

....

....

....

....

....

....

....

....

....

....

....

Stress Free ✒️

Stress: pressure, strain, anxiety, constant worry, nervous tension, trauma, hassle, wrung-out! Sound familiar? A busy schedule, a hectic personal life, relational problems, an overburdened work life, mental conflict, words that keep tripping you up and emotions either in a state of dire neglect or spinning out of control while your mind continues to live in denial! This is a recipe for having a resentful approach to your daily life. You press on relentlessly hoping that your body's warning signals of stress and burnout might simply take leave of their own accord. They never do. Part of the process of your restoration is to recognize that your life is valuable, precious and in demand. You need to understand God's order and realize that you first need to love and take care of yourself so that you don't give the fragmented leftovers to Him and to those in your family, in your place of work or your other areas of responsibility. Loving and caring for yourself is not a luxury, it is an absolute necessity. You cannot help but appreciate and care for yourself when you see the price Jesus paid to redeem you, not only from sin but from yourself. Value yourself enough to give yourself quality and quantity of time. Spend time in His Presence and know His rivers of refreshing. He is the Well that never runs dry. He is your Haven in the midst of the storm. It is all a matter of getting your priorities in order. It really is about personal choice. You see, the Source of all life is God the Father, through Jesus His Son, working through the Holy Spirit. If you neglect Him in the plans of your day, your days will find you defeated, hopeless and lifeless. He is the One who can and will sustain you in the multifunctional and multifaceted roles you must fulfil. He is the One who understands the pressures and demands like no one else can. He is the One who is calling you to come away and be with Him for a while. In His Presence there is fullness of joy.

Creating a quiet space and time in your busy day can revolutionize your entire week.

I have seen lives torn apart by worry and anxiety. I know the results. Fear and anxiety were companions in my life for far too long. They are destroyers and do your life a great deal of harm. One of the most comforting Scriptures I meditated on day and night during those years was 2 Timothy 1:7, *'For God did not give us a spirit of timidity (of cowardice, of craven and cringing and fawning fear)'*, *but He has given us a spirit of power, and of love and of calm and well-balanced mind and discipline and self-control.*

Lord, when I am burnt out, infuse me with the light of the Holy Spirit.

I received this prayer via email some years back and I know the power of its potential:

Lord Jesus, as I enter my new day, I take Your Presence with me. I speak Your peace, Your grace and Your perfect order into the atmosphere of this environment. I acknowledge Your Lordship over all that will be thought, spoken, decided and accomplished within these walls. I thank You for the gifts You have deposited in me. I do not take them lightly but commit to using them responsibly and well. Give me a fresh supply of truth and beauty on which to draw as I do my work. Anoint my creativity, my ideas and my energy, so that even my smallest task may bring you honour. Guide me when I am confused. When I am weary, energize me. Lord, when I am burnt out, infuse me with the light of the Holy Spirit. May the work that I do and the way I do it bring hope and courage to all that I come in contact with today. And O, even in this day's most stressful moment, may I rest in You. Thank You Jesus that You are with me even when it seems I am not with myself!

There is a very powerful key to being stress free:

> *'But seek (aim at and strive after) first of all His Kingdom and His righteousness, (His way of doing and being right), and then all these things taken together will be given you besides. So do not worry or be anxious about tomorrow, for tomorrow will have worries and anxieties of its own. Sufficient for each day is its own trouble.'*
>
> (Matthew 6:33,34)

Yesterday is gone and can never be lived over again. Tomorrow is not yet your reality. So go ahead, make the most of today! What good can it do any person to worry about yesterday if you cannot change but only forgive the past? What good is it to worry about tomorrow when we don't even know what the next hour holds? Your life needs to be placed in the capable and loving Hands of an all-knowing God. Confronting the way you feel about circumstances and life allows you to do something about it. It is often when you ignore the warning signals of physical fatigue and mental exhaustion that the tiny acorn becomes a giant oak tree which then needs serious uprooting before it overshadows every part of your life. If left unchecked, this giant can often result in one having to use anti-anxiety medication, undergo therapy or be forced to recover from a nervous breakdown. There is no time like the present to set time aside, yes even in your busyness, to list those issues that cause you to fret, whether they be shadows from your past, circumstances that impact your present, or issues that cause you to fear your future.

To stand tall in a falling world, it is imperative to your sense of wellbeing that you learn to live in the present to extract the most out of the moment.

As part of your restoration process, it is imperative that you start at the very foundation of your existence. Examine your life. Conduct an excavation procedure, dredge up the sludge and create a clear shaft for your thoughts, your words and your actions to be released. Have a spring clean and once and for all throw out the chaos in your life, so that you can live the life you were meant to live and not one that is dictated by your unresolved issues. When you begin to see yourself as God sees you, the way that He made you and the purpose for which He designed you, your perception of your life will change. How you live your life in this moment determines the way you make entrance into your next moment. Live your life in bite-size digestible pieces.

To stand tall in a falling world, it is imperative to your sense of wellbeing that you learn to live in the present to extract the most out of the moment. Your mind and body must occupy the same space at the same time. Be focused and connected with what you are doing at one moment in time. Guard against your body being on remote control while your mind considers other matters and your emotions take you to places you don't want to be. Positively seizing the moment; being in alignment – spirit, soul and body – is one of the catalysts to having victory in the days ahead. Your destiny is created moment by moment. Your journey is your destination. Enjoy the journey. You may wish to get to 'where the grass is greener', but there is a lot of lawn to mow there too! Enjoy where you are. It's a powerful key to being stress free.

> *It is not the strongest of the species that survive, nor the most intelligent; but the one most responsive to change.*
>
> CHARLES DARWIN

To stand tall you have to resist inflexibility to changing circumstances. Your aim should be to become and remain pliable in the Master Potter's Hands. You must, for your own benefit and for those with whom you live and interact, be flexible. Life is, quite simply, not perfect. Change is constant and change is here to stay. Change is here today. If you are often disappointed because certain plans or situations do not work out the way you would like them to, this can be a stumbling block to your restoration. You will live with the mindset that you won't try anything new or trust in anything just in case it disappoints you again.

> *Trust is a choice; an act of faith.*

Disappointment comes from not having your expectations met. Unmet expectations are part of life and the sooner you accept the fact that life is challenging and everything will not necessarily be the way you would like to have it, the less stressful demands you will make on your own life and on others. It is wisdom to agree with your circumstances, knowing that every circumstance is offering you another lesson in life. Learn from it. Recognize that you do not always see the eagle-eye view and in many cases had you insisted on having your own way you could have forced open closed doors and might have ended up with a dilemma far greater than you could handle. Trust Him Who knows the end from the beginning.

There is peace in knowing that there are Divine Delays. This is a principle in life worth nurturing. Many times this knowledge has saved me from having to resort to crisis control. When you can get to the place of yielding and surrendering to the Lordship of Jesus Christ, you can know for a certainty that He is in total control, despite how you feel. Your life can then be lived with joy in your current circumstances. Trust is a choice, an act of faith.

You don't need to go somewhere to be free, you can be joyful and free where you are. Freedom too is a choice made in faith. Have faith in a faithful God! There have been many times I'm sure, when you have tried to walk around, perhaps ignore, or have even tried to climb over your circumstances – anything but go through them! It is by going through them in surrender and trust that you overcome, grow and rise in stature and experience. What is sent your way is often what you need. Trust God with your future, your career, your destiny, indeed your life. This call to surrender is not easy in anyone's estimation, but I am learning that He is worth surrendering to. The only way you will know you have overcome a situation is when you are faced with the same situation time and time again. When one has truly overcome, there is no impact or reaction to a circumstance, and in truth, no projecting, pretending or strategizing. You will find that you are at peace and stress free when you are not moved by what you see or what you feel.

Martha served the Lord. Mary touched the Lord.

God will not expose you to anything unless He has a significant purpose for you to experience and learn from the circumstance. He is the Master Planner. I have often wrestled with God on this one. There is so much suffering in this world – how can I ever understand its purpose? Maybe I never will. What I do know is that His ways and knowledge are beyond my finite understanding and His plans far more complex than I can comprehend. In it all I know that He is God and He loves me and I can trust Him with my life. Take a moment to consider the times when you have tried to push open closed doors or have ignored those Divine Delays. What price have you paid to have your own way, as opposed to enjoying the rewards of trusting in the timing of all-knowing God?

Have you ever contemplated that your ceaseless activity and forcing circumstances could be related to your need for affirmation? Do you believe your busyness could equate to you feeling valuable? I am reminded of two women, both with noble intentions, but only the choice of one of them returned a substantial reward. Both Mary and Martha had the Guest of all guests in their home – Jesus. Martha chose to allow her perfectionist, 'if I'm busy I must be valuable' attitude to have full rein as she mindlessly raced around attending to this and preparing that, dipping into the conversation now and again. Mary, however, chose to touch Jesus with her presence in a quiet and attentive way, acknowledging that her Guest was worthy of her full attention. Mary could arise from sitting at His feet knowing she had accomplished more in that time than Martha could have accomplished in weeks of frenetic striving. Martha's spirit, soul and body were divided. The outcome of this was that she projected her frustration at her sister who was in the process of having her beauty restored in the Presence of her esteemed Guest. Martha served the Lord. Mary touched the Lord.

All too often I meet people who are bowed down with the weight and pain of carrying unresolved issues, just like Martha. My aim is to conduct my daily life in such a way that as each circumstance arises during the course of my day, I deal with it there and then, first within myself, allowing my thoughts to clear, my emotions to settle and my spirit to be unhindered. I then allow myself time to ensure that I do not react out of anger, hurt or frustration. It may call for a period of time to pass before the appropriate moment to raise the issue with the person concerned. The main

Stress is the price we pay when we haven't paid the price to prepare.

principle, however, is that I deal with myself first. If I am the injured party, it is my responsibility to resolve it. This has got to be one of the hardest challenges for any human being because the protective mindset is usually, when I am in pain, the one who hurt me should feel it! Trying to get even raises your stress levels to even more dangerous heights! A powerful antidote to stress is having and exercising self-control.

Standing tall in a falling world requires that you order your life aright, ensuring you truly live all the days of your life, and disallow the daily issues of life to overwhelm you. Talk about how you feel. Both talking and writing about what you are experiencing or feeling are both very therapeutic. Just be sure that the person you are speaking to is one you can trust and who isn't one of 'Job's comforters' and condemns you for feeling the way you do. Eating healthily contributes greatly to combating stress in your life. Excessive salty foods raise your blood pressure, which, added to your stress, can be a fatal combination. Ensure you are getting good restful, peaceful sleep. Clear your mental 'inbox' and de-stress your mind before you go to sleep. Reading something that relaxes you is a comforting way to enter into peaceful sleep. Exercise is essential as a stress reliever and if you listened to your body carefully enough you would hear it pleading for exercise and movement. Exercise causes you to breathe deeper than you normally would without exercise. Check your breathing and your posture. This will tell you much about the stress levels in your life. Short, shallow breathing and poor posture are indicative of stress ruling your body. It is very important to be on time from the moment you wake up. Every minute you lose in the morning will compound in time lost as the day progresses. Living stress free takes time and discipline. Make stress-free living a part of your lifestyle. You will be glad you did.

My Reflections on Living a Stress-free Life

I am Habit

'SIMPLICITY IS THE ULTIMATE SOPHISTICATION.'
LEONARDO DA VINCI

I am your constant companion.
I am your greatest helper or your heaviest burden.
I will push you onward or drag you down to failure.
I am completely at your command.
Half the things you do, you might just as well turn over to me,
And I will be able to do them quickly and correctly.
I am easily managed; you must merely be firm with me.
Show me exactly how you want something done,
And after a few lessons I will do it automatically.
I am the servant of all great men
And, alas, of all failures as well.
Those who are great, I have made great.
Those who are failures, I have made failures.
I am not a machine, though I work with
all the precision of a machine
Plus the intelligence of a man.
You may run me for profit, or run me for ruin,
It makes no difference to me.
Take me, train me, be firm with me
And I will put the world at your feet.
Be easy with me, and I will destroy you.
Who am I?
I AM HABIT – AUTHOR UNKNOWN

It seems it's time to dream again
Both wide and very high
It seems it's time to dream again
And be great before I die
It seems it's time to dream again
Of empires great and vast
It seems it's time to dream again
Of something that will last.
It seems it's time to dream again
And accept God's Sovereign will
It seems it's time to dream again
And move from being still
It seems it's time to dream again
And build my life anew
Yes, it seems it's time to dream again
Yes, it's time for you and me to dream again.

AUTHOR UNKNOWN

My Reflections on My Habits

Chapter Three

Standing Tall in Your Relationships

Relationships – Our most basic need in life is relationship. God never intended for us to live or work alone. Life is all about having good, workable relationships. Relationship-building should become a strategy for life. Our lives are 100% relationship-based. From the moment you were conceived you commenced your life-relationship journey.

The most influential relationships are forged in your formative years and progress into your adult years. Every relationship you have ever formed has played a part in influencing your life to some minor or major degree. If your relationships are out of sync, you are out of sync, and this can result in complications in both your personal and work life.

Amongst your most important relationships in your life is the relationship you have with yourself! You spend more time with yourself than you do with any other person. Your relationships should be your greatest and most valuable of assets! Accept and develop a great relationship with yourself. Remember it is not someone else's responsibility to make you happy. Commit to personal growth, development and change, so that you can be a better person for someone else to be in relationship with.

Reviving Your Relationships ❧

WE EXIST BECAUSE OF RELATIONSHIPS.

Our most basic need in life is relationship. We don't really know who we are until we are in a good, healthy relationship with ourself, and then we can confidently share our life with others. Our lives are 100% relationship-based. From the moment we are conceived we commence our life-relationship journey. The most influential relationships are forged in your formative years and progress into your adult years. Every relationship you have ever formed has played a part in influencing your life to some degree. If your relationships are out of sync, you are out of sync, and this can result in complications in both your personal and work life. Two of your most important relationships in your life are firstly the relationship you have with God, and secondly the relationship you have with yourself. The stronger your relationship with God, the more wonderful your relationship is with yourself. The overflow from these two relationships becomes a pleasure in the lives of the others that you relate to. You spend more time with yourself than you do with any other person. It's a great idea that you really like being with yourself. Your relationships should be your greatest and most valuable assets!

I, not events, have the power to make me happy or unhappy today. I can choose which it shall be. Yesterday is dead, tomorrow hasn't arrived yet. I have just one day, today – and I'm going to be happy in it.

GROUCHO MARX

Make it part of your daily focus to accept yourself and foster a great relationship with yourself. Commit yourself to personal growth, development and change so that you can be a better person for someone else to be in relationship with. Never look to another human being for that which you must first find within yourself. No one human being can be all things to another. Many people live unfulfilled lives because they constantly seek for someone to make them happy. The truth is it is not anybody else's responsibility to make you happy. Many believe that people are the source of their lives and that is why they live in continual disappointment. The right order is to acknowledge God as the Source of your life and embrace people as the gifts in your life. When you receive a gift on any occasion, you always accept it graciously and with thanksgiving. The same appreciation should be shown to those people who are the gifts in your life.

Learn from the mistakes of others. You can't live long enough to make them all yourself.

ELEANOR ROOSEVELT

Knowing that God is the Source of your Life is the catalyst to being confident in loving yourself as He loves you. After all He created you and He has a purpose for you being you! Not being comfortable with who you are or who you are becoming can lead to the most awful sense of loneliness. It sends you on a no-hope journey of trying to find someone else to fulfil you, and when they don't you become even more uncomfortable with yourself.

Conduct edifying relationships and put a stop to the energy-sapping and life-sucking relationships that don't add value to you but rather rob from your life. Remember, however, that no relationship remains constant. We all experience ups and downs, the good and not-so-good in every relationship. This is a natural part of life and provided you use each experience as an opportunity to learn and grow, you can avoid making the same mistakes again. Wherever and however you can, preserve your relationships – don't sever your networks or burn your bridges; you never know when you may need to be in relationship with that person again!

The most important contribution we make to any relationship is not what we say or what we do, but who we are and who we are becoming. The most powerful relationship we can humanly experience on this earth is the union between a man and a woman. It has been said that the man is the head but the woman is the neck – a vital support for the head! It is vital in the building of successful, workable relationships that you value the differences in others and resist the division that can often be created by the differences. In learning to love yourself, love others – your spouse, your children, parents, family and friends. Love is the greatest gift you can share with them. Don't control them but release them to be all they were created to be. It is after all not your job to try to change or improve others. At best you can be an influencer and motivating factor in their lives, so that they can be inspired to begin their own personal process of change. Remember that when you convince someone against their will, they will still be of the same opinion.

Story writers say that love is about young lovers and the excitement of romance. This, they believe, ends at the altar. That is the lie we have been sold and have believed. The truth is the most wonderful romance and the greatest love stories are found inside the marriage. The lasting legacies come after the marriage, not before it.

Submission was never given to reduce potential. Submission is an act of love and it brings protection. Godly submission brings out fulfilment in a woman. The husband can only fulfil his covenant obligation as the woman submits to his headship. This act of submission is a demonstration of a woman's love for Christ and her husband. The marriage ring is a symbol of love and life, not a claim to domination. How marriage partners treat and respect one another is how they will treat God. Submission is not an act but a choice. Like is a feeling. Love is a decision. One may not feel love but a choice is made to redeem love. Women who do not know how to yield become very tough, rebellious and often cruel. There is nothing stronger in the world than gentleness. People will always respond positively to a gentle and quiet spirit. A quiet spirit is not a wishy-washy, spineless doormat, but exudes a quietly confident approach. A quiet spirit is not demanding of attention, brash or haughty. We need to have the right spirit to create the right environment for relationships to blossom. Submission is a partnership, a 'going-under' – pursuing the same mission together. Marriage, it has been said, can be the closest thing to Heaven or to hell.

Make a marriage-transforming decision today to bring your relationship closer to Heaven.

However if a marriage is closer to hell than it is to Heaven, it may well be time to make a different choice. Marriage was never designed for abuse, undermining, control or despair. When a marriage is in the destructive cycle of control, manipulation and domination, it requires change. Only you know the change you must make to be at peace with yourself and others. The success of any relationship is dependent on both parties 'joining together'. Both partners have to commit to the requirements the unity demands.

My Reflections on My Relationships in My Life

Become a Transformer 🌿

Transformation at a personal level releases potential within you that can be translated into increased productivity in all the vital areas of your life. Transformation begins with the need to change. Without acknowledging the need and receiving information that change must take place, there is usually not enough reason to embark on the process of transformation. Transformation requires dramatic change and that change can be costly and painful, but it does work for your good in the long term. Transformation demands that we have the information made available through others that gives us messages that we need to change. These messages often come in the outworking of our relationships, whether at home or in the workplace. Very rarely is there a requirement for people who live in isolation to make any dramatic shifts in their lives, because quite simply, they are living for themselves. So, unless you are planning to spend the rest of your life on a deserted island, you will be given messages through circumstances or people that you need to make some changes. As an example, these messages are reinforced when you perhaps exhibit an annoying habit that your spouse has overlooked for some time, but finally he/she reaches the point where he/she can no longer tolerate the habit. The result is either you change the habit or the relationship changes in one form or another. It may be that the person who reports to you is continually late for the start of work or for meetings. Sooner rather than later, you will no doubt give the message that the behaviour needs to change. Should the person not change the behaviour, it will result in them losing their job. If you don't honestly address the issue, you will be the one with the ever-increasing frustration.

Unless you are planning to spend the rest of your life on a deserted island, you will be given messages through circumstances and people that you need to make some changes.

The revelation that nothing is going to change until you make a change needs your ownership; your seal of approval on it. Unless you make the choice to change, most of life becomes an imitation, a fabrication or frustration; living your life without true conviction and commitment to your personal values, standards and boundaries. Ultimately this leads to stagnation in your life. Nothing changes, nothing moves, nothing grows. Transformation is a productive process. You simply cannot stagnate when you are in a constant state of transformation. Transformation is the antidote to imitation. Imitation arises when you believe you cannot be the originator of a new idea, or be resourceful or innovative. Imitation is following someone else, whereas the transformation process is the catalyst for a person with a pioneering spirit and future outlook to make significant changes to the rest of their life, and then become an influence in the lives of others. Since our Creator God is the Real Originator we can never run out of ideas, insights and concepts to create and bring forth something that was never thought of before. Unless you change how you are, you will always have what you've got. Just take a moment to consider the fact that everything you experience materially in the world today was once someone's original thought. There is no limit to the power of creative thinking that is birthed out of personal transformation, which results in freedom from self-limiting beliefs and past experiential baggage that can weigh you down, and stifle your creative thinking.

Through the process of deep personal change, one is able to recover what might have been lost in relationships. Because when you are transformed, your perceptions change and you begin to see things very differently. Furthermore, you take responsibility for the mistakes you made in the past and forgiveness is more readily released. Relationships then stand a real chance of being restored. How often have you heard of a situation where a couple have got divorced and, because the divorce was the message that change was required in both parties, it became the catalyst for each party to undergo their own personal transformation? With the perfect science of hindsight from the viewpoint of their newly transformed way of thinking, they look back and reflect that if they had known then what they know now, they would never have got divorced. This is why it is so crucial to listen to the messages you receive even on a daily basis to encourage your personal transformation. When you make a habit of asking yourself why you have received specific information, you can skilfully use that information to apply dramatic changes to your life – your way of doing and seeing things. This personal transformation process can save your job, your marriage, your life!

True transformation starts by taking full responsibility for your own life. When you take this level of responsibility and embrace the changes and outcome of your own life, you can become a transformer in the lives of other people and encourage them to undergo the same process. They will thank you for it.

My Reflections on Becoming a Transformer

Today I make the commitment to myself to be courageous enough to hear the messages that come across my path from the many different people in my life, that can bring about transformational change, so I can start living the life I was designed to live.

Face Reality ✍

KNOWLEDGE WITHOUT APPLICATION IS MEANINGLESS INFORMATION.
DENIAL LEADS TO DEFEAT.

When you have heard something, you have to make a choice about what do with it and when you know what to do, you have the responsibility to do it. The longest distance in the world is between what we know and what we actually do with that knowledge. The biggest gap in our life is between knowing and doing. Someone once said, *'If we all did what we know to do, we would all be skinny, rich and happy!'* It is time to reinforce the need to get out of denial and face reality if you really want to experience effective and lasting change in your life. It is having the courage to come face to face with where you find yourself in the present, and armed with those facts, you can then apply common sense to the situation, and establish a plan to take you onto the next level of desired change.

> *'For if anyone only listens to the Word without obeying it and being a doer of it, he is like a man who looks carefully at his [own] natural face in a mirror; For he thoughtfully observes himself, and then goes off and promptly forgets what he was like.'*
> (JAMES 1:23,24)

One of the reasons people stay in the destructive cycle of crippling debt or bad relationships, or they continue eating unhealthily or not having an exercise routine, is that they choose to live in denial and hope it will all smooth out along the way, instead of facing head-on what needs to be challenged and changed. It is the pain-pain-pleasure principle that Anthony Robbins often refers to. You discover, for example, that you have gained 10 kilograms over the past year. That is painful! However, the truth is, it is going to take another type of pain to get back into shape. This is the pain of eating less, eating healthy foods, starting an exercise programme and, most importantly, sticking to it. You will only be able to pay the price of this pain if the pleasure is really worth it. The pleasure will be felt in having greater confidence in your appearance, wearing clothes two or three sizes smaller, feeling the elation that comes with the ability to discipline yourself and being able to harness those cravings. This pleasure then becomes a way of life. Making the right choices today means no regrets tomorrow. Personal growth and development is not an option. Don't wait for crisis to force you to bring about change in your life. You make the decision to design the kind of life you want to live and, with persistence and diligence, you will reap the harvest that comes from sowing the seed of good-quality choice.

> *Everything that does not move you towards success moves you away from success.*
>
> ROB RUFUS

Every human being has internal assets and liabilities that can help or hinder their lives each day. The assets such as unleashing your imagination and creativity, being positive in your outlook, igniting new ideas and concepts and gaining helpful insights into situations, having the courage, boldness and tenacity to implement these ideas, combined with your skills and talents that are resident with you, are assets that have invaluable worth. These assets should be what we focus on each day, and the very spark that we keep fanning into flame. Liabilities on the other hand, are those traits that you must of necessity face and deal with, but not focus on, otherwise they have a tendency to rule your life negatively. Liabilities can be small-mindedness, pettiness, dislike of self, anger and frustration, being intolerant or impatient, being controlled by perfectionism, having continual fear and anxiety, being lazy or being poorly organized. These hindering negatives have to go so that the scales can be brought back into balance and you can capitalize on your assets to take you to the place you really want to be in your life. Living with enhanced and valuable assets will hasten you towards your personal success.

> *Face reality and choose the life you want to live.*

Gone are the days when doing your best was good enough. The bar is continually being raised in many aspects of this life, and what was considered to be brilliant two years ago may just be mediocre now. Just ask Olympic athletes. The level beyond doing your best is taking ownership of the mindset that says, 'I will do whatever it takes.' If you want to experience satisfying relationships, are you prepared to do whatever it takes to be fulfilled? If you are overburdened by debt, are you willing to do whatever it takes to get out of that destructive cycle? If you are bored and not stimulated in your work, are you going to waste your valuable 24 hours per day doing what you dislike or are you going to do whatever it takes to risk a change? Remember nothing much is going to change until you decide to change it. One of your life's mottoes must become, *'If it is going to be, it must certainly be up to me!'*

No idea is ever executed without the plan first being laid. Yet having a plan and not putting action to it is equally as ineffective. Focus on what is really important for your life and start with the obvious. Are you willing to pay the price, and are you prepared to do whatever it takes? There are no shortcuts to achieving the meaningful things in life. Everything nice has its price. The end result may take longer than you had anticipated, but stay the course. Never give up on your ideals and dreams. There is a harvest if you do not faint in the process. Let your reward be what others thought to be impossible. Face reality and choose the life you want!

My Reflections on Facing Reality in My Life

Communication that Brings Connection ❧

In today's pace, this is an everything-in-a-second-world, where instant communication seems to be the name of the game; what with eye-zapping, flashing luminous billboards, televisions with fridges wrapped around them bellowing out the world's dreary news while we cook our meal in a minute; teens zoned out – in tune with their iPods and out of tune with their studies, and the day's bull or bear financial trading results at the push of a button on our laptops or mobiles, causing one's day to rise or fall, depending on the performance of the markets. Not to mention a quick SMS for someone special who has a birthday today, or popping an email to your next-door neighbour who you know has not been well for some time. Whew, I feel exhausted just writing about this stuff. There is no denying that the pace of technology has made our world an easier place to communicate and to transfer information, but it certainly hasn't facilitated relational communications. Much personal communication which should be discussed face to face, eyeball to eyeball, kneecap to kneecap in honesty and openness, has been hidden behind typed and veiled messages, leaving the recipients to wonder if they ever knew what the sender was meaning at all.

When the pressure mounts in the household and the tension becomes unbearable, what easier way to deal with it than to hide in the television? Better still, pop in your music player earplugs and drown out the world. Who cares what your wife or husband has to say, anyway? Dinners around a family dining table are almost unheard of today, because after all, what would we say to each other when technology has been saying it all for us? What would a meal

How can you find ways to best communicate with each other to bridge the great divide?

be without the family glued to the gazillionth episode of yet another reality programme? And yet, amidst the constant chaotic download of information, the hurly-burly of advertising screaming for your attention, and an offer of another chat- or date-line that promises to spice up your life, you find the world a very lonely place. That is because we have truly lost the art of connected communicating.

When last did your eyes engage with someone with whom you were seriously and attentively in conversation? And I am not talking about sexual conversation. Someone to whom you really took the time to thoughtfully and respectfully listen? A conversation that has the richness of contribution, learning, listening and responding? A dialogue that goes beyond giving pat answers and the glib 'yes' and 'no' at the appropriate places. When last did you seriously take an interest in what your spouse was so desperately trying to share with you? How long ago did you meaningfully ask a question with genuine interest, and not just because it was the required thing to do? If you have ears to hear in this cluttered world, relationships can become far more meaningful, mistakes will be avoided and you could find yourself exploring the depths of conversation and communication like never before.

I am beginning to discover that developing in life really begins with asking questions. The greatest inventors in this world refined their ideas by asking a series of questions that led them to the answers they needed to complete their inventions. A physician cannot treat a patient until he has asked the questions that will give him answers to assist him in his analysis. Sound, fruitful relationships are built on learning about the people in our environment and the way we learn about them is to ask them about their lives. I have been astounded in my work with people who have failing marriages, how little people know about their partners. It is little wonder to me then, why they have no idea where to start working to salvage the relationship. They have never taken the time to understand why their partner reacts a certain way. They do not stop to ask what, where, when, how? They may be in a marriage but not in a relationship. Marital breakdown is often first a communication breakdown. It stems from living in the same house with someone whom you really don't know because you don't sincerely communicate. Oh, you talk to each other, but neither communicates to learn about the other person or to try to understand who they are and what has made them who they are. How can you find ways to best communicate with each other to bridge the great divide?

Communication involves your spirit, soul and body. Love is expressed through relationship. Relationship is supported by communication and relationship can only grow to the degree you spend time communicating and sharing. The truth about relationships is that there will come a time when the ecstasy phase is over and there will be conflict along the way. As always, however, you have the choice whether you communicate destructively and eventually head for the divorce courts, or you communicate with restoration in mind. Where good-quality communication is lacking, there is no closeness. Where there is no closeness there is no foundation for conflict resolution. There is no middle road in relationship communication. Break the connection through destructive communication and you break the connection of intimacy. Constantly reacting in a destructive manner will cause serious, long-term damage to your relationship.

When there is a communication breakdown, your self-worth can be damaged by the words and actions of your partner and vice versa. Disconnection in communication births disunity.

> *'The disunited household will collapse.'*
> (LUKE 11:17, AMP)

When you have been hurt by your partner's lack of sensitivity in communication, you close off your soul – your mind, your will and your emotions – which results in detachment and withdrawal. This ultimately becomes the barren land of lack of sexual intimacy and emotional connection. Affection is the barometer of the condition of a relationship. United in relationship means that U and I are tied. Break that unity

When someone can cause you to react, they have power over your life.

and you break that connection. Love as you want to be loved. Sow love to reap it. Sow good communications to reap the same. Regain hope for your marriage today because you will have to live through it tomorrow. But, it has to work both ways. Both partners must commit to the requirements that unity demands.

Communication is a process we go through to convey understanding from one person to another person or a group of people. When people complain about a lack of communication, they are also saying that there is a lack of understanding. Ensure that your hearer understands what it is you are saying. It's not necessarily what you tell someone that they hear, but it is more about how you say it. What is the emotion behind what you are saying? A person of understanding holds their tongue. Remember this life-changing truth – when someone can cause you to react, they have power over your life! Never complain about someone or a situation unless you are prepared to confront the person or situation. Otherwise this, over time, becomes another source of destructive communication.

Reckless words wreck relationships.

In a conflict situation try your very best to avoid criticism and judging. Address the behaviour that has been displayed and don't attack the person. Avoid saying words like 'You never' or 'you always...' As difficult as it is, try not to take the conflict personally and remain calm and dignified. Keep your tone low and your stance non-aggressive. Engage your brain in the communication and keep your emotions controlled. Don't speak recklessly but always speak the truth in love. Reckless words wreck relationships.

The written word and the spoken word are the most powerful human forces on the earth. Communication is the lifeblood of every relationship and organization. You are best received when you present yourself with a warm, welcoming and sincere attitude. Make people feel good about being around you. Remember that listening is 80% of the communication; only 20% is speaking. 100% communication is when speaking – or answering – completes the cycle of listening. When you ask a person you meet for the first time a number of interesting questions about themselves, they will leave your presence remarking that you are one of the finest communicators and most wonderful people they have ever met. Such is the power of interested listening! **Standing tall** in a falling world means doing whatever it takes to become a skilled, refined communicator.

> *'One of the most healing human acts is also one of the easiest to accomplish. The act is one of listening. Listening creates relationship; it helps us connect to others. People do not always need an answer; they sometimes just need to know that someone cares enough to listen. The individual with the greatest influence will be the greatest listener.'*
>
> JOHN PAUL JACKSON

My Reflections on My Communication

Significantly You 🕊

YOU ARE YOUR MESSAGE!

If there was a way to measure the number of years we have spent wishing we could look like someone else, have someone else's talents, legs, height or hair, I think we would be astounded. It stems from societal conditioning through the media glossies that having a 'certain look' is a must. My husband and I have often discussed that seeing someone attractive, whether male or female, is not about whether they just have nice eyes or a great smile, but it is really about the whole person, the entire package. That package may even be carrying more weight than they would like, or perhaps the person may feel as though they have had a 'bad hair' day, or they have got out of the wrong side of the bed, but nevertheless, because they have an intrinsic confidence that they are significant and uniquely created, they make a powerful impression. The truth is… You are Your Message.

Brands power the world. We live in a society that is driven by brands and many mistakenly believe that brands give them their identity. It is powerfully satisfying to know that our true identity is found in Christ Jesus. Everything we were ever designed to be is found in Him:

> *'But you are the ones chosen by God, chosen for the high*
> *calling of priestly work, chosen to be a holy people, God's*
> *instruments to do his work and speak out for him, to tell*
> *others of the night-and-day difference he made for you –*
> *from nothing to something, from rejected to accepted.'*
> (1 PETER 2:9)

Our brand, therefore, is the brand that reflects a changed and significant life; one that enables us to step out and put our best foot forward. A brand is a particular make of something or someone that displays an identifying trademark or label, and this brand is designed to impress unforgettably. Your entire life speaks louder than you will ever realize.

Each day of your life you are in the process of building your particular, unique personal brand in spirit, soul and body. Jesus paid the highest price anyone could ever pay to redeem you to Himself – you can stand tall when everything else seems to be caving in around you, confident in the Brand of His powerful redemption. Your life will be a representation of the life of Christ in you. Since your real identity is found in Christ Jesus, your personal brand is distinctive. Your level of self-worth can be at the highest peak because you can value yourself as one that has been bought with the highest price, and you are loved. The way you see yourself – your self-image – can be displayed confidently, not arrogantly.

> *Your brand is what people say about you when you are not in the room.*
>
> JEFF BEZOS, FOUNDER OF AMAZON.COM

'God says you are the head and not the tail;
you are above and not beneath.'
(DEUTERONOMY 28:13)

Your confidence can soar to new heights because you are seated with Christ in Heavenly places.

'It's in Christ that we find out who we are and what we are living for.
Long before we first heard of Christ and got our hopes up, He had
His eye on us, had designs on us for glorious living, part of the
overall purpose he is working out in everything and in everyone.'
(EPHESIANS 1:11,12)

Knowing this truth – put your best foot forward and smile. There is nothing more inviting than a warm and friendly smile. A smile exudes confidence. Positive eye contact says more about you than it does about the person you are looking at. Your eyes are the window of your soul – let His light shine through them. Let everything you do be founded on the values that God has set for you to walk in.

The message of your life is spoken not only in words, or by your opinions or your contributions, but daily; moment by moment, you are giving your message to the world because of who you are and how you present yourself. We actually get only one chance at making a significant first impression. Life is really a series of presentations. The better your presentations are, the better your life could be. Stop for a moment and think about your daily presentations to your husband, to your children, your colleagues, your employees – to the world. In truth, you are modelling life for your children and for those following your leadership. What impression are they left with? All of life is an experience. The reason people go back to the same restaurant, clothing boutique or business suppliers is because, in the main, the continual experience is a good one. Daily we are giving people experiences… are they coming back for more? Your impression on someone is created within a few short seconds. In every presentation you make, people are buying you first! When you greet a person or engage in conversation with them, make them feel as though they are the only person in your whole world! Children especially crave that undivided attention from their parents. If we would just give them the amount of time they require, with no distractions and no diversions, we would find that they would skip away more content and less demanding the rest of the time. Your significance is more than just the way you look, although looking great plays a vital role in how you feel. How you feel about yourself is measured by your self-worth. How much do you really value yourself? Do you appreciate yourself and are you thankful that you are you? The way you see yourself determines the way you will live out your life, because who you are dictates what you see. If you feel great about yourself, you will more than likely have wonderful things to say about other people and you will view your world very differently. When you have a correct self-image

> *Life is really a series of presentations. Life is experience.*

> *Example is not the main thing in influencing others. It is the only thing.*
>
> ALBERT SCHWEITZER

you can beam with self-confidence, being assured that you are created and loved by God, and that you are walking in His plan for your life, and it is good!

> 'He creates each of us by Christ Jesus to join Him in
> the work He does, the good work He has got ready
> for us to do, work we had better be doing.'
>
> (EPHESIANS 2:10)

The thoughts that you hold about yourself and your world are of vital importance to your significance in life. Right **perceptions** display great projections. A projection is what you give out in communication and body language. Right perceptions also give you a wonderful **reception**; an ability to receive what others are saying about you. Someone can give you a compliment and you are able to receive it without apology. Many wonder how they can become more successful, have greater wealth or become happier. The answer lies in becoming a more successful, wealthier and happier person in your heart and mind. Happiness and success are things we should be attracting, not only pursuing. A more significant you may just be one choice away. Do what you can, with what you have, where you are.

Do what you can, with what you have, where you are.

THEODORE ROOSEVELT

Many of you reading this may be of the opinion that you don't really have what it takes to make an impact or be powerful in who you are, but I want you to be encouraged with this:

> 'You may not think that the world needs you, but
> it does... For you are unique, like no one that
> has ever been before or will come after.
>
> 'No one can speak with your voice, say your piece,
> smile your smile, or shine your light. No one can
> take your place, for it is yours alone to fill.

'If you are not there to shine your light, who knows how many travellers will lose their way as they try to pass by your empty place in the darkness? Use your one life to make a difference in your world. Become the change you want to see in the world.'
MAHATMA GANDHI

The world is not really the way it is; it is the way you see it. You have your own ready-made set of filters through which you receive, feel and approach the world. These filters have become part of the reality of your life. What you perceive to be truth for you, whether actually true or false, will be your reality. The way you see yourself, your ability to contribute to those around you, to make a difference in this world, and the way you conduct yourself, all determine the outcome of many of your life's experiences. Holding wrong perceptions about yourself and others means that you will most likely not be confident in projecting yourself well. Remember, the new you is but one choice away! Make the shift. Reject the negativities and wrong perceptions and replace them with the positive limitless possibilities that you can live into.

Thinking

If you think you are beaten, you are;
If you think you dare not, you don't;
If you'd like to win, but you think you can't,
It's almost a cinch you won't.
For out of the world we find
Success begins with a fellow's will –
It's all in the state of mind.

If you think you are outclassed, you are;
You've got to think high to rise,
You've got to be sure of yourself before
You can ever win a prize.

Life's battles don't always go
To the stronger or faster man,

STANDING TALL IN A FALLING WORLD

But sooner or later the man who wins,
Is the one who thinks he can!
ANONYMOUS

Only **you** can give excellent expression to your life by being confident, content, and by making a contribution, sharing who you are with others as often as you can. When confidence and contentment within yourself are lacking, one can tend to become insecure and introvert, and their expression to the outside world is one of being aloof, unapproachable or distant. Only you can make the change and difference that needs to be made. The fabric is already on the inside of you. There is not something external that can be poured into you to make you any more content or confident. Rather, it is that something special that needs to be released from within you, to influence the people and the environment around you. Make a decision today to step out of your safety net and dare to make a contribution to someone else's life and see for yourself the reward that comes from that. A bottle of fragrance needs to be opened to release the benefit within. It's the same with you. Take the lid off your life and spread your fragrance around the world. It needs you!

Find creative ways to become in demand and gain 'more market share' in your environment. Perhaps it is time to change something that you have been saddled with for too many years to remember; that 80s hairstyle, the clothing from yesteryear, a concrete, inflexible way of thinking? Make who you are indispensable. Make people want what you have to offer. Know your value and your worth, and recognize it in others. See yourself the way you want to be. Dig deep to discover all that trapped potential. Potential is your power in reserve; that which has not been tapped into as yet. Unleash that potential that is hidden under the 'I wish I could, I wish I was, I'll never be able to do that, they must be much better than me…'. Try new ways of doing things even if it is scary at first. Persist, persevere and don't ever give up. You are so worth it.

Everything you need to be successful and significant is already on the inside of you. You just need to learn to let it out. One more added anything is not going to make a difference to your life until you first release what you already have. Only you can give excellence to all your expressions in life. It is you and you alone that can make the transition from mediocrity to magnificence.

It is you alone who can make the choice to go from mediocrity to magnificence.

You are, after all, your major asset. Look the part without saying a word about who you are. Let your significance and uniqueness ooze with confidence and purpose. Never apologize for who you are. Go prepared to market yourself before you market your product. Take your value to the marketplace, not your need. The higher peoples' expectations are of you, the more they will positively draw out of you.

In the pursuit of significance in your life, if you are aiming to do anything well, you should aim to communicate well. Communication is the lifeblood of every relationship and of every organization. It is important to remember that we are always communicating. Even though you may not be saying a word, your eyes tell a story, your posture speaks volumes, the set of your face discloses much of what is taking place on the inside. You are communicating 24 hours a day, every day of your life. Have you noticed you never have to tell someone you are happy, sad or angry? People sense it a mile away!

Standing tall in a falling world calls for you to lighten up, travel lightly through this life and leave the baggage behind. Don't become a 'master baggage handler', trying to keep under control those things that are threatening to overwhelm you; rather clear away the clutter, release it and replace it with living abundantly in the present and having anticipation for a powerful future. Focus on your significance rather than on your imperfections. Be conscious of yourself enough to be sure of what you have to do, but don't become tripped up by self-consciousness. This is when you are overly

May your life be filled with abundant blessings, unmatched significance, great favour and overall success.

aware of yourself to the degree that you cannot engage with others significantly, because you are too worried about what they are thinking of you! Always remember, enthusiasm will give you a significant life presentation that will profoundly impact others. There is nothing more refreshing than being with someone who is enthusiastically comfortable with who they are. They are significant!

My Reflections on Being Significantly Me

Never Lose Your Awe for Life ❧

Some years ago my family and I went on a fun-filled holiday to Disney in Orlando, Florida. It was so interesting to gain insights through the experiences that we enjoyed; insights that were quite an eye-opener to our daily routines of life. The first experience that impacted me was how dangerous excess in any arena in life can become. Balance in all things is, for sure, one of the major keys to living a fruitful life. There is no doubt that excess leads to consequences that may well be near impossible to rectify. Instant everything and instant gratification has resulted in a 'been there, done that' approach to life and has brought on depths of boredom that have robbed life of its element of surprise. It is amazing in the age in which we live, where the wonder of technology is escalating at a rapid rate, communication is more intense than at any other time in history, and new inventions, discoveries and cures are the order of the day. These things are so fascinating and creative and yet life in all its awe can be such a yawn for so many. The day we lose our awe for life is the day we lose everything. What comes after that? You see, awe is not found in experience alone, or in money alone, nor in adrenaline rush alone. Awe is found when you believe in the awesomeness of your created life, in the One Who created you, in the awe of who you are and who you are becoming. Experiences of life then should fill you with much joy.

Death is not the greatest loss in life. The greatest loss in life is what dies inside us while we live.

NORMAN COUSINS

Being a partaker of the fun at the theme parks brought home many realizations. The enormity, sheer creativity and imagination that is behind every detail in, say, the Magic Kingdom or Sea World reminds one of the absolute necessity of never stagnating in who we are or what we do. We can never in one lifetime achieve everything we are capable of because the possibilities are limitless. Re-invention should be top of your mind so you avoid the ruts and routine which can so easily rob the colour from your life. Always be creating space for greater growth and development. Never accept your current achievements as the norm. Don't be limited by believing you have reached your ceiling or your shelf-life date. Disney is going to achieve for decades to come… why can't you? Don't let your age or your ruts in life deceive you into believing you cannot achieve what you really want to achieve. There is no end to what can be.

Walking around the theme parks, standing in one-hour-long queues, and jostling onto all the rides can be a most exhausting experience, while fun all at the same time. Often in life, people give up way too easily and quickly because 'their feet hurt'. In this business of life, if you really want to achieve what you have set out to achieve, you need to press on despite the pain, whether physical, mental, emotional or financial. You have to push past weariness. Don't focus on what hurts, focus on your goal.

> *Opportunities pass, they don't pause.*
> ANONYMOUS

Focus on the reward that will come from achieving your goal. You will reap a harvest if you do not faint in the process of waiting and expecting.

When you get onto the roller coaster of your business, your relationships, your plans or your dreams, remember that once you are strapped in, once that harness is secured, that signals your 'commitment to the process'. You cannot be whizzing around at 65 miles an hour, 90 feet off the ground and decide that 'this is not for you'. Stay the course, stick to the process, find joy in the journey and don't let yourself or anyone else interrupt your journey because of *their* fear of *your* adventure.

Never lose your awe for life, the awe of what you see happening around you. When you lose your awe for life, you lose your passion for life. When you lose your passion for life, you lose your excitement and when you have no excitement, you cannot self-ignite or self-motivate. All that remains is that you become a spectator of life, not a participant. When people don't participate you will usually hear comments such as, *'Success only seems to happen to some people. Nothing ever seems to come my way. Tried that before and it never worked. I can't help it; it's just the way I am.'* Jim Rohn says, *'No longer be frustrated but turn your frustrations into fascinations.'* Rather be fascinated than frustrated. Fascination comes when you realize what YOU really can achieve despite the obstacles!

Passion, excitement and self-ignition are the boosters to launch your personal rocket. Where would you like to go? What would you like to experience? It is going to mean you need to strengthen your inner person to be tough and resilient. It means not quitting when the challenges become tough and terrifying at times. It is about **standing tall** to slay the giant in your land. It will mean regaining your awe for life. Becoming excited again at the prospect of what can be. Arising in awe will awaken you to what can be. It will provoke you to capitalize on every opportunity in life; for opportunity passes, it does not pause. Be confident enough to take the risk to get out of your rut. Make up your mind to be optimistic and courageous, to work hard and achieve your personal goals. You will become more insightful and perceptive as you learn to follow your instinct and your expectation in life.

> *'Many people don't recognize opportunities when they come*
> *their way. These are often the type of people who complain*
> *about the noise when opportunity knocks at the door.'*
> ANONYMOUS

My Reflections on Living with Awe

✧ Today is the day to start living with awe! Any delay today can stall your momentum.

✧ Exchanging your yawn of life for the awe of life can change the rest of your life!

Experience and Confidence ❧

THERE IS NO AMOUNT OF MONEY IN THE WORLD THAT CAN BUY CONFIDENCE.

No amount of money or even trading in your most valuable possession would ever be able to obtain experience and confidence for you. Experience and confidence become two extraordinary possessions when you begin to realize their true worth. This is why it is so crucial that parents do not intercept their child's ability to 'learn the hard way', which is not to say that one must be cruel to be kind, but rather in order not to stunt their growth in the experience and confidence departments, allow them to grow from feeling the consequences of disobedience and dishonesty, for example. It is important that they be allowed to take risks to grow in confidence and be able to formulate a basis for decision-making that will be required later in their life. If you constantly intervene and make their decisions for them, they will not develop the life-skill of assessment and evaluation, which translates to making a decision based on their own assessment and then being able to act on that decision. If they are not allowed to trust their own judgement and instinct they will always be relying on someone else to make their decisions for them. The decision-making may be from a peer group, or an undesirable association, that make disastrous decisions in the absence of their own self-assurance, and this could have lifelong consequences.

Experience is a high-price-tag item. Only those who have the attributes of persistence and determination will be able to enjoy receiving the rewards that experience brings. Experience demands stick-at-it-ability, it means going back to a previous place of frustration or to a circumstance where you have been knocked down. It requires facing the giants in your life, sometimes a hundred times over, like the flawless gymnast working at a floor routine until the pain threshold has been broken; until the routine becomes a part of her and a new level of experience can be chalked up on the board. A trainer or teacher can reiterate eternally about how 'it' should be done, but it is only when you have personally done 'it' and worked at 'it', can you claim to have experience in 'it'.

Experience and confidence go hand in hand. The more experience you have, the more confident you become. The more confident you are, the more you are willing to grow in your experience. I have seen this first-hand with my son who is totally focused on the extreme sport of wakeboarding. Wakeboarding is like being on a snowboard, except the wakeboard is pulled behind a high-powered boat and tethered by a rope and handle, at the end of which he confidently performs somersaults, sky-high jumps, tumbles and spins, while my inexperience and lack of confidence in this arena cause my nerves to jangle. His little dabbling on a wakeboard some years

> *If you will spend an extra hour each day of study in your chosen field, you will be a national expert in that field in five years or less*
>
> EARL NIGHTINGALE

ago, coupled with determination, pushing aside personal fears and pressures, and breaking through the pain barrier of a damaged knee, water slaps, having the wind knocked out of him, and bruised ribs on many occasions, has turned into a professional endeavour, with a focus to develop even greater skills and compete at an international level in a very extreme sport. If I, however, had my way I may well have intervened when he was at a younger age with the caution that the sport is too extreme and dangerous and that it would be safer to 'stay in the boat'. Just how much experience and confidence would I have cost him, I often wonder? This would have been to his detriment. I now watch how he has formed a strategy for his own life from his experiences as a wakeboarder. He tackles life fearlessly, confidently and is always willing to take a calculated risk. His experience has caused him to be adventurous and curious. All of these attributes are required of someone who will be leading and be responsible for others.

The take-away value is this: when you pay the price, take the risk, break through the barriers of self-limitation or limitations that others have put on you, there simply is no ceiling to how experienced and, therefore, how confident you can become in the things to which you put your mind and hand. There is no substitute for first-hand experience. Consequences are one of life's greatest teachers. This is why when you try with all your good intentions to pour your heart into a conversation with your teenager about what they shouldn't be doing, or who they shouldn't be going with, because in your experience such and such happened, they look at you with a pitiful look as if to say, 'Well this is not my reality.' It is vital that they be allowed to carve out their own reality so that they can take ownership of their lives. The only way they will learn

Consequences are one of life's greatest teachers.

their own lessons is by having their own experiences. They will be more confident and decisive as they learn first-hand what not to do, and what to do more of to get the results that work for them. Ouch! Now, as parents, we would be so happy for them not to have to endure the pain that experience brings, but if they don't have their own experiences they will never know the potential of what can be – for good and for bad. And if all they have as evidence is your say so, it will always be a temptation to try. Getting your children to stand tall in a falling world may require letting them fall now and again so that they know how to get up again!

It is worth 'getting out of the boat' to gain enriching life experiences.

My Reflections on Experience and Confidence

Transformational Leadership 🕊

'LET THE GREATEST AMONG YOU BECOME AS THE YOUNGEST, AND THE LEADERS AS ONE WHO SERVES.'
THE WORDS OF JESUS

All of life is essentially relationship-driven. Leadership is relationship at its peak. Your life experiences have a greater potential to influence people than mere theory or academic knowledge. People love people who lead by example and not by directive and dictate only. A person in authority, with positional power, can demand that change takes place in an individual, either in their attitude or performance. The subordinate can comply either cheerfully or maliciously. The authoritative approach in leadership, however, never guarantees internal change – only compliance. A leader who has influence and personal power can effect substantial change in another person because there is no demand made, but rather a powerful invitation to embrace the opportunity to walk together and jointly make a positive contribution. People feel empowered when they are invited to exercise their freedom of choice. The individual's levels of self-esteem, personal value and worth are elevated when they aren't autocratically forced into making changes, but are rather partnered in the progression of making internal changes that create successful external outcomes. Companies spend untold fortunes trying to raise leaders by equipping them with more information, when, if they rather approached leadership fundamentally as relationship-building and mentoring, they would reap greater results in commitment, contributions made and increased productivity levels. Internal transformation is the key to having external impact, as nothing really changes until an individual changes from the inside, and only then can they effectively influence their external environment.

The challenge for leaders in any decade is that human beings are fallible and imperfect and they are continually impacted by life experiences. These experiences are then exhibited in a variety of ways on a daily basis in the workplace. The fall-out of these experiences can be reflected as negativity, malicious compliance, absenteeism, lethargy and inefficiencies. As a leader you can have the best intentions, the most profound experiences, the greatest knowledge, Harvard graduate leadership skills and be a powerful communicator, but in the end, the challenge is that you are dealing with people who will ultimately make their own decision whether or not they will follow you. It has been my experience that people will follow

The brilliant leader always brings their people face to face with their potential.

a leader who cares, who understands that leadership is about relationship and not title, and who will give them a sense of belonging and assistance when their world is falling. Every day one comes across highly talented people with the potential to make a valuable contribution, but the level to which that person rises will always be determined by themselves. You can have the utmost belief in a person's ability, but unless they take ownership of it for themselves, your belief in them will only assist to a point. The leadership challenge then is to grow people from the inside out, helping them to see themselves as being able to make a valuable contribution, to reveal their potential and to give them an avenue to release that potential. Some years back the Dale Carnegie Institute conducted a research programme with 50 CEOs who represented 50 Fortune 500 Companies. Amongst the questions the CEOs were asked was what they believed their employees wanted to experience from their companies. Their comments were interesting; however, they only addressed the external requirements of the people. They believed their staff wanted good salaries, opportunities for promotions and job security. What was really interesting was that when they interviewed the managers and staff who reported into these CEOs, the results were somewhat different. The staff answered that they wanted verbal and experiential recognition for their work. The staff wanted and expected to have a sense of belonging; being part of a family, and they wanted to be recognized as people who faced some difficulties in life, not just people who had skills. Furthermore, they wanted sincere appreciation shown to them. It is also interesting to note that the World Youth Organization recently conducted a survey among young adults entering the working world. The findings were that the organizations and type of leadership that would attract the emerging youth of today would be companies who would give them a purpose for going to work each day, something to believe in, and hope for the future. Perhaps if leaders took cognizance of the results of this type of research they would see increased levels of productivity and greater pride being taken in the workplace. Nobody wants to just do a job!

Being a leader is not an act but rather a lifestyle. The character of a leader is the beacon light that draws people to them and a truly successful leader is one who attracts followers rather than pursues them. Character is what a person is when no one else is around. Leadership has four foundational pillars: integrity, trust, honesty and wisdom/good judgement. Making wise choices cements the future of a leader because you produce after your own kind. What you sow is what you reap. An essential quality for leadership is credibility, not perfection. Who is following you? Who are you developing? How do they experience your leadership style?

> *Management is doing things right. Leadership is doing the right things.*
>
> PETER F. DRUCKER

Good leaders have the ability to bring out the very best in their people, inspiring them to do their tasks with excellence but at the same time helping their people to fulfil their personal purpose. I believe an organization can never over-invest in the personal development of its people because people give meaning to the organization. An effective product without effective people to promote the product is a futile exercise. People who are being transformed at a personal level give impetus to productivity and boost the potential of any organization. As a leader beware of limiting others because of your own limitations. It is imperative that in order to strengthen your leadership, your life must constantly display self-development disciplines and personal management as the norm.

Women as Leaders

Marilyn Monroe said, 'I don't mind living in a man's world as long as I can be a woman in it!' She was right. Women are being given opportunities that were once only afforded to men. Jealously guard your womanhood and do not be deceived by the lie that you need to become like men to get the job done. With the current window of opportunity that is set wide before women, make it your aim to work at becoming wiser. Women were never designed to stride in the footsteps of men. You may need to negotiate around new situations that will arise from having two demanding careers in the household and children who have valid needs, but it is up to you to create an environment that is conducive to ensuring that your career doesn't tip the scales to the detriment of your relationships. Women are at their most powerful, influential and successful when they are living out their most natural womanly traits. Women run the risk of wearing the labels of 'impossible boss', 'more aggressive than her male counterpart', 'totally unapproachable and tough', and 'hard as nails!' It is sad but true that many women, when afforded the opportunity to rise to a level of authority, believe they must shed their womanly behaviour and take on male characteristics that were never intended for them in the first place. Being female is a matter of birth but being a woman is a matter of choice! The power that is invested in your womanhood can be maximized in your position of leadership. You don't need to trade roles to get the job done.

Any organization is not a complete organization without women. Women were never created to compete with men, but to complete them, and this works not only in personal relationships, but also in business relationships. Women have a variety of gifts, skills, talents, passions and services that can add value to an enterprise. Because women intuitively have insight into many situations, their

> *Leadership by force cannot endure.*
> *Leadership by Influence leaves a legacy.*
>
> ANONYMOUS

123

decision-making processes may not always be as conventional as they are for men, but they are usually very accurate. Women bring the influence of spontaneity, because they usually consult with their hearts first, before they engage logic and reasoning. This adds a feminine touch to the male boardroom environment and coupled with a woman's inherent care and compassion for people, empathy, and a nurturing spirit, every organization benefits from the fact that women are essentially relationship-driven before they are task- and productivity-driven. The balance, therefore, within any enterprise between men and women leaders is a very delicate one. Both groups are needed for their individuality and their corporate synergy. Women are quickly emerging as a new breed of leadership. Transformational leadership is more about lifestyle than it is purely about function. Being a significant force in your world of business does not require changing who you were created to be. You may have to shift some attitudes and approaches, but never at the cost of your womanhood. As many women are quickly emerging as leaders in the world, they need to guard their womanhood zealously. Women are at their most powerful, influential and successful when they are simply being the women they were created to be.

Leadership is designed essentially to move people, ideas and organizations from one level to the next. What better way to lead than to build workable, trustworthy and dependable relationships with those whom you want to take to the next level? If we cannot relate to others, we certainly cannot lead them. Not relating to a group of people you are supposedly leading can quickly turn to autocratic rulership which then, in turn, breeds a rebellious culture within the organization. On the contrary, leaders who are leading through relationship-building are inspiring, encouraging and facilitating of changes within the organization. This is powerful in an organization, because your people feel that they are respected, appreciated and are invited to make a contribution. It has

Life-Leadership before People Leadership. Relationship before Function.

124

been noted in recent research that one of the major reasons why people move from organizations is because they no longer feel they can make a contribution, or that their contributions are not appreciated. The need for people to be able to make a contribution is clearly seen in many who have had successful careers and then suddenly retire. Often within two years or so, they find themselves in ill-health, or dying, because their sense of being able to make a valuable contribution has been removed, particularly if they have no other areas of interest in their lives.

Somebody so wisely said 'Leadership by force cannot endure. Leadership by Influence leaves a legacy.' Leadership is indeed a combination of character and strategy. If you have to choose one, choose character. Strategy can be learnt but character can never be bought. It is generally known that Bill Gates believes in employing for attitude above skill, because skill can always be learnt but a good attitude cannot be bought. The mark of good leadership is when you move from 'me to we', recognizing that your leadership is not about you alone, but it is for others. So what is the responsibility of the Transformational Leader? To lead another is to go in front or to guide. Because you are leading the way, be sure that you see things right before you attempt to set things right. Shift your perspective if need be. Challenging your perceptions about the people you are leading is all-important since you will be directing their actions and opinions.

Leadership is really about pioneering, preparing the way and setting the course for others to follow. The characteristic of a good relational leader is one who knows their identity and is confident in it. An insecure leader is ever in danger of feeling undermined and threatened, and constantly questions their own abilities. One result is that their management style is defensive, hostile and demanding.

Being an effective leader starts from within.

Good leaders have unquestionable credibility and integrity for they know that once trust has been broken, it is one of the most difficult things to restore. Trying to lead people who don't trust you is like pouring water through a sieve. It has no containing power. When you are trusted it becomes a greater platform for you to display your ability and competence. Trust inspires your team's support as you pioneer with fearlessness, perseverance and determination. Humility is one of the most vital characteristics that you can display and that people can experience. Humility opens the door for you to be teachable, to learn from those who are making a contribution; to love people and conduct quality relationships. Arrogance has to do with position. Humility precedes true power and influence. Arrogance is about perverted authority that forces people into things. The outworking of this in employees is usually malicious compliance, resentment and disrespect for the leader. Strong, quiet confidence from a leader births influence that invites people to change and perform at a higher and more effective level. That is not to say that humble leaders are soft touches or pushovers because that is not true leadership either. Because of their quiet confidence, humble approach and unquestionable character, they have the power to have honest, open and meaningful confrontation when necessary, creating a culture of trust, confidence and respect.

Humility precedes true power and influence.

Transformational leadership is an inside-out approach. It is relationship-focused vs function-focused. The relational leader always brings their people face to face with their potential, helping others see the big picture and not just part thereof. Remember that as a leader you are always dealing with people who need someone to love, something to do and somewhere to look you never thought possible. There are many definitions of leadership. Everyone has a different opinion about what good leadership is. It is hard to describe – but you certainly know when you have had an experience with a brilliant leader.

The transformational leader understands that leadership based on effective relationships is the leadership that is going to stand the test of time and leave the most powerful legacy. We cannot lead others when we cannot even lead ourselves. Being an effective leader starts from within. The making of a strong life-leader is how that person responds to their own life's experiences – that can either shatter or strengthen them at a personal or professional level. Someone who has endured the trials of life and has overcome is well capable of leading a group of people and helping them to see themselves as better than they are. The compassionate leader is able to inspire others to rise up in more than their daily work, even in the outworking of their lives.

Leaders are the transformers of business, government, education, the entertainment world and society. To transform means to make dramatic changes. The transformational leader understands the need to move from 'me' to 'we'. This leader is not afraid to bring others along with him because he is secure in himself and not threatened by the contributions made by others. True leaders give of their significance into the lives of others. They are done with the autocratic bullying and demanding that things get done or that people comply. Instead they invite contribution, reasoning and dialogue. Leaders can truly only be powerful as they share their personal power with others.

The quotation by Jim Rohn underscores that Relational Leadership is anything but weak. True leaders will have to practise tough love on those who choose to resist or defy their leadership.

Choose this day whom you will follow, because your leader is sure to lead you some place. Be sure it is the place you wish to be.

'The challenge of leadership is to be strong, but not rude;
be kind, but not weak; be bold, but not bully;
be thoughtful, but not lazy; be humble, but not timid;
be proud, but not arrogant; have humor, but without folly.'
JIM ROHN

My Reflections on My Transformational Leadership

✧ Are you following a leader who aligns with your values?

✧ Does your leader inspire confidence, security and trust in you?

✧ What value can you add to your leader?

The Creative Leader ✒

The world is powered by imagination. It takes a smart leader to be a creative leader. The smart leader will recognize that if he taps into his own creative abilities and the imagination and abilities of others, the vision will be reached in a reduced amount of time. Limiting creativity is limiting your life, your people's lives and your organization's potential. Creativity costs nothing to release, but it costs everything to lose. Losing fabulous and inventive people results in a massive loss of potential, productivity and profit. If you as a leader don't harness the creativity available to you through others, those who work with you will become frustrated and use their creativity elsewhere. Use them or lose them! Encouraging the contribution of people's creativity can boost productivity beyond your wildest expectations. Creativity can be expressed in the most menial of tasks and is not only something that is required to power the brands of the world. Each person is so unique that they hold a different view and perspective to you. Capitalize on this and make it work for you and for the overall objective. Inviting people to share their creativity is inviting them to trust you. Creating trust begins with the leader. Trust stimulates confidence and commitment. Commitment is a choice of the person you are leading. Creating an environment of trust and contribution allows your people the freedom to express their creative ideas without fear of rejection. Broken trust leads to frustration, a lack of motivation, loss of focus and the end of unity.

> *Limiting creativity is limiting your life.*

Encouraging the contribution of people's creativity can boost productivity beyond your wildest expectations.

Unity is built on the principles of honesty, openness, integrity and commitment. Honesty is the open door to sound relationships. Trust is birthed out of honesty. The day you become dishonest with someone you destroy trust. Openness creates an environment of sharing, contribution and vulnerability. You want people to operate from there so that their creativity can be released. Integrity says, 'I am who I am – all the time. I have no hidden agendas. What you see is what you get. I can be trusted'. Commitment means that you are not dependent on your circumstances to be a certain way before you will commit, but rather you are directed by your internal values. You do something not because someone else expects something of you, but because you expect that high standard of yourself. Commitment never compromises. Being committed to each other and being in unity means that you all contribute towards making the vision a reality and a success.

> *An essential quality for your leadership is credibility – not perfection.*

> '*I believe that being successful means having a balance of success stories across the many areas of your life. You can't truly be considered successful in your business life if your home life is in shambles.*'
> ZIG ZIGLAR

An essential quality for your leadership is credibility (trustworthiness, integrity, reliability and sincerity) – not perfection. Be believable, truthful and honest and people will be able to trust you. People must be able to trust you or they won't be able to follow you. The litmus test in your leadership is whether your character can stand on the pillars of flawless personal values, strong moral fibre, your balanced and predictable temperament and the constancy of your disposition. The well-known Bible teacher, D.L. Moody, stated that '*Character is what a man is in the dark.*' When no one else sees you, when you are on your own, when you are alone with your thoughts; in that secret place, who are you? Conduct the mirror test. Look at yourself honestly and ask, 'Is it right, is it moral, is it

> *The eager listener will be the brilliant leader.*

legal?' If you cannot answer 'yes' to all of these, then don't do it! If in doubt, don't! Nothing destroys the credibility of a leader more than the lack of personal integrity.

Capacity is to have the mental and physical ability to conceive, to perceive and to have the energy to sustain the outcome. It is being able to have the emotional capacity to stand under the responsibility of leadership. The more powerful a leader you desire to be, the greater the capacity you must have.

Great leadership calls for great capacity.

Effective communication is one of the driving forces of effective leadership. The leader who can communicate personably, professionally and with intent and care, is the leader who will produce the most effective results. The eager listener will be the brilliant leader; the one who gains understanding and insight before commenting is the one who will be listened to and whose advice will be taken. Communication can be the downfall of a leader when they lack the sincerity to praise others, and only comment on their mistakes, or become overly critical, instead of rewarding their people for creativity and for attempting something new, even if it means making mistakes along the way. True leadership is about looking more often in the mirror to check yourself, than looking through a magnifying glass to see what others may be doing wrong. It is worthwhile remembering that you are not only a leader in the workplace or in your organization, but in the home too. Your spouse and children will respond well to great leadership displayed in gestures of appreciation, kind comments and in inviting their contribution. Are you who you say you are, all the time?

The enemies to your leadership are when you become indifferent and inattentive to people, and are more focused on their outputs and results. Richard Branson says that the secret to his success is in taking care of his people. His people take care of his clients – and the profits take care of themselves. Indecision and procrastination is a killer to your leadership. You will miss the in-the-moment opportunities, and your competitors will get in ahead of you. Qualified and well-thought-through decisions need to be made today, not tomorrow when the opportunity has passed. Worry and doubt will overwhelm you if you

> *To give real service you must add something that cannot be bought or measured with money, and that is sincerity and integrity.*
>
> DOUGLAS ADAMS

don't check it when it comes in through the door. Whatever is pushing you, you need to push back! Leaving worry and doubt to fester will weaken your leadership and your decision-making. You cannot operate in faith and fear at the same time. One will always be a slave to the other. Make sure your fears are the slaves to your faith! When you are faced with a new horizon in decision-making, don't look at it as though you are standing at a crossroads, which can make you feel more confused. Rather see yourself standing at the threshold; the dawning of a new day; a door to a new opportunity. Step over in faith and confidence. Enjoy the vista!

My Reflections on Creative Leadership

✧ What relationships need to be repaired in order to raise your level of creative leadership?

✧ In what ways can you create an environment of trust, unity and commitment?

Marriage at Work 🌿

'MARRIAGE IS A MICROCOSM OF LIFE. MARRIAGE IS A REFLECTION OF WHAT WE PRACTISE OUT IN THE WORLD, IN OUR LIFE AND IN THE WORKPLACE.'
ERNEST DU TOIT

As life is a balancing act, it is crucial to find the balance in your spiritual life, your physical and emotional wellbeing, your family connectedness, your business or workplace success, your intellectual fulfilment and your social life. The values in life and marriage are, among many others: commitment, loyalty, dedication, peace, unity, harmony, passion, reliability, dependability, consistency, character, wisdom, sound judgement, purpose, vision and goal setting. The characteristics that detract from life and marriage are, among others: aggression, disloyalty, inconsistency, lack of dedication, aggravation, frustration, disunity, unhappiness, spitefulness, jealousy, enmity, foolishness and unwise decision-making.

You cannot be in right relationship with another person until you are in right relationship with yourself.

In marriage, as well as in the workplace, it is not about finding the right marriage partner, or finding the right job, it is about being the right person for the marriage or for the job. Firstly, this comes about by making the choice to be the right person for your marriage partner or to be the right employee for the company. Secondly, it is by growing within yourself, being prepared to pay the price for unity, within the context of your relationship, that will give you the return on your great investment. You cannot be in right relationship with another person until you are in right relationship with yourself. You need to be the very best *you* you can be, to give the very best *you* to another.

Right relationships almost force us into accelerated personal growth and development. You cannot be interacting with someone at an intimate level without being challenged to assess your personal development. If you are reacting to situations the same way you did ten years ago, you will continue getting the same results in your relationship and work environment that you did ten years ago. The choice is quite simple – we either continue exhibiting negative behaviour patterns and get the result of destruction in relationships, or we change. As John Maxwell says of his employees, 'Unless you change, I'll change you.' In other words, he will replace someone if they are not prepared to move up to the next level, review their attitude or develop in a certain area.

Who am I becoming that I might make others more powerful?

BENJAMIN ZANDER

Every human being has to find equilibrium in the balancing act of life. Every day you juggle many balls in the different roles you play. Imagine that all of these balls are made of rubber and can bounce back to you. All, except your relationships. This Relationship Ball is made of crystal glass. If you drop this ball, it cannot bounce back to you. So precious is a relationship, that you should treat it as the most valuable of crystal glass.

If you make all your decisions from a place of love, then you will never again make a wrong choice.

RACHAEL BERMINGHAM

The evidence of personal growth and development in your life is when you can break out of old paradigms – old ways of thinking – when you can truthfully break with the past and live in the present with great expectation for the future, when you can embrace the processes that change brings, and when you can inspire your partner to grow. Most importantly when you can live a life of transparency, openness, honesty and vulnerability, and peace which leads to unity. Unity aids growth, encourages greater wisdom, and the exercising of sound judgement. The more we grow at a personal level, the more we can apply these principles in the workplace. We can only add value to our place of work to the degree we are growing at a personal level.

Marriage is the perfect training ground for growth. It provides a practice arena for personal relationships, the result of which can be expressed in the business and wider world. Life is all about relationships. Business is about relationships, and when this is understood it leads to better business practice. Fulfilment comes through partnership – not command and control. Women were meant to complement and not compete with their partners. Equal partnership means sharing and counter-balancing each other's strengths and weaknesses. Equal partnership is creating the environment where each individual can thrive. It is empowering, enabling, complementing and brings out the best in each other. Equal partnership releases positive performance, appreciation of each other, and the freedom to contribute.

Equal partnership means sharing and counter-balancing each other's strengths and weaknesses.

If employees are immature in their personal relationships, it is reflected in the workplace where the attitude becomes one of more demand, the mindset being 'What is in this for me? What can I get out of this?', and therefore less value is added by the employee. Right relationship once again becomes the basis of effective output. If we are going to be 'We' I must first love 'Me' because when I love me, I can comfortably share my life with another. As you grow and develop at a personal level you are able to take those whom you lead to a new level, both personally and professionally. Never underestimate the power of your personal influence. No relationship remains constant and as you reach new platforms of personal leadership you should become increasingly effective in dealing with the inconsistencies that arise in relationships at all levels. The most important contribution you can make to any relationship is not what you say, or what you do, but who you are and who you are becoming. The more value you add to a relationship, the more in demand you become. You determine the quality of relationships you wish to live through, both in your personal and professional life.

'One life stamps and influences another, which in turn stamps and influences another, on and on, until the soul of human experience breathes on in generations we'll never even meet.'

Mary Kay Blakely

My Reflections on My Relationships

✧ It is never too late to regenerate a relationship.

✧ Take that decision today to do whatever it takes to enjoy the relationships that you desire at home and in the workplace.

Chapter Four

~

Standing Tall in Your Daily Life

Daily Life – Every person on earth has 24 hours a day. 24 hours in which to choose whether life works for them, or against them. It is true that life mostly consists of routine. It is also true that your life will be determined by the attitude you adopt in the midst of the routines that frequent your daily life.

Living a victorious life every day is going to require that you know your why for life. What makes you *you*? What makes you want to get up in the morning and do what you have chosen to do? Or do you even want to get up in the morning? Successful daily living is about making the choice to make the most of the seasons of your life – the winter and the summer; the magnificent and the mundane. Dynamic daily living is about expressing gratitude, developing excellence in your life and becoming alive to the possibilities that surround you every moment of your life.

Finding the balance in your daily life will also help you to feel more in control of your 24 hours. Empowered living every day requires making empowering choices and making the choice to avoid derailing yourself with self-defeating thoughts, words and actions. Every day holds within it invaluable possibilities. How are your viewing and experiencing your daily life?

What is Your Why for Life? 🌿

Today is life! This moment in your life is the one and only moment you can be sure of. How often do you take time to step off the treadmill of life and take your focus off all your roles to simply stop; to reflect and contemplate and to consider how magnificently and uniquely you have been created? Embrace this truth: of the six billion people on the earth today, there is only one you. Never before in the history of mankind has there been another you, and long after your footprints leave this earth, there will never be another you! You have ability, purpose and destiny designed in your very DNA. You are a never-to-be-repeated-again masterpiece. It is time to celebrate you. Celebrate your contribution to the world. For it is only in making a contribution to the lives of others that you begin to experience true fulfilment in your life.

> *You have ability, purpose and destiny designed in your DNA.*

Fulfilment is experiencing the sense of accomplishment, achievement and contentment that comes from the pleasure and joy of living life with a bigger-than-you purpose. There is nothing quite as frustrating as investing in a piece of equipment that is designed for a specific purpose, only to discover that it cannot fulfil its purpose nor reach its full potential. Take for example, an iron or a kettle, or even a motor car. You make the investment, having a full expectation that the iron, kettle or motor car will give you the return you expect, only to find that, for one reason or another, it cannot fulfil the purpose for which it was designed. Regardless of how technologically advanced and wonderful these creations are, if they cannot fulfil the purpose for which they were created, they cannot warrant their usefulness. Effectiveness is

> *Transformation requires dramatic change that first demands a dramatic shift in your thinking.*

the basis for true success. Effectiveness is realized in fulfilling the purpose for which you were created.

True success is not so much about what you have obtained or achieved, but about who you are, and who you are in the process of becoming. How effective and purposeful is your life? It is making the transition from being busy, busy, busy to get more, earn more and have more, to becoming a person of substance and significance. The significant person is the one who applies their life's learnings not only to their own life but to the lives of others, and who gives of their wealth and resources for the benefit of others, while enjoying the fruit of their labour with gratitude.

Being continually success-to-excess-driven means that your attention is totally focused on your own desires and achievements. It is all and only about your performance. Now, aiming for success, of course, has its place, and it is a strong driver within most human beings. However, being successfully significant requires that you share what you have achieved with others, as an overflow of who you are. Quite simply, you cannot give what you do not have. People with a 'me' focus never go beyond themselves and in the end their takeout is very empty.

The secret of success is constancy to purpose.

BENJAMIN DISRAELI

The 'success-to-excess' mindset can lead you continually to push yourself too hard and you become dependent on the accolades of others, resulting in you not being able to step off the treadmill, even for just a moment. For, like an addict, you begin to base your successes on what others say; your ego demands their continual feedback and you are pressed to pump up your performance to keep the accolades coming. You therefore have to work harder to keep yourself satisfied and sacrifice the quality of your life and relationships on the altar of other people's approval. Transformation

Your life is what you think it is.

calls for dramatic change. Dramatic change is what is needed to break the relentless demands that keep you running when you know it is time to stop and redress your life. Find fulfilling ways of building into the lives of your spouse, your family, your friends and those who require your valuable contribution. It is when you make the shift from striving and performance for everyone else's approval, to appreciation of your life, that you start to really enjoy your life. In his book, *Finishing Well*, Bob Buford shares, by way of interview, the stories of many high achievers who found that their lives never really became significant until they realized that life wasn't only about their achievements or their own wealth creation, but it certainly was about using what they had learned, gained and achieved to add value to the lives of others, whether by way of mentoring, financial support and helping them to start their own business or venture into a new career.

Your thoughts and your words create action.

We have been miraculously created to reach our full potential in this one life we have been given. Yet so few recognize or release their powerful potential; instead it is often leaked out in the pursuit of that which offers paltry profits. One of the definitions of potential is that it is your latent power waiting for release. Many go to the grave with much of their powerful potential still unused. There are no sadder words of tongue or pen, than the words, 'It might have been.' Life is too short to live or die with regret. It has been said that some of the richest land on earth is where the graveyards are situated. Many have died with all of their wealth on the inside of them, not releasing their talents that should have been their gifts to the world; gifts of music, art, poetry, dance, hospitality, business, education, politics, writing novels, sharing of wisdom, gifts of creativity and of speech and film-making.

There are many reasons for trapped potential: fear, a lack of confidence, the restrictions that painful past experiences bring, and unbelief are just some of the enemies of your potential. Unexpressed feelings never die; they merely express themselves in more harmful ways. This is one of the reasons people are driven to overachievement, to burn out; and why they are in desperate need of the approval of others. Emotions become misplaced, and unresolved matters get entrenched in hard work, long hours and unrealistic expectations. The result is that relationships suffer, stress levels soar, fatigue and general disinterest in life become your portion. Only when you know what you want out of your life, will you know what you need to put in. It is an unchangeable truth that what you sow will become your harvest. What harvest are you reaping in your life? Too many people live lives of quiet desperation, secretly hoping that someone, or circumstances, in their life will change. They do not realize that, resident within them, are all the ingredients to make the kind of choices that will begin to mould and manufacture the very things they so desire.

Your life is what you think it is. How you think totally affects your life. Thought is the seed of all experience and action. What you think in your heart will be expressed outwardly. Focus your thoughts on what you do want, not on what you don't want. Anything you want to see different in your outer life, you must first see in your inner life or imagination – your thought life. Whatever is impressed in your thoughts will be expressed. Steffi Graf, who was the women's reigning tennis champion for a number of years, gave the secret to her game. 'I keep my eyes fixed on the tennis ball.' She went on to explain that her concentration is so refined that while she is playing the game, she can actually see the lettering of the company that manufactures the balls. Not the movement or the reaction of her opponent, or even the crowd, affected her game. Her mental focus was fixed on one object – and that was the secret to her success. How do you define success and how can you achieve that success and keep the balance in your life?

You are always communicating. Communication is evidenced in your facial expression, your attitude, your posture, your body language and in your verbal communication. Your thoughts determine your feelings, which translate into your attitudes; your attitudes are expressed in your words and your words create action. What you 'see' in your mind's eye is usually what you get. Most of our problems stem from wrong thinking. Imagine if Steffi Graf focused on the crowd and not the ball.

To stand tall when your world is falling, you owe it to yourself to find out your 'why' for your life and to value yourself enough to leap off the hamster wheel that takes you around in circles. Give yourself valuable time to de-stress your life and allow yourself to stop… breathe, and be thankful for the awesome life you have. It is time to begin to reach out to other people, to value them, and share your significance with them. Share all those awards, accolades, successes and finance with those who may not have experienced the privileged life you have known. This is your 'Why' for life. One day when your life ends it will not matter whether you have saved billions, built mansions or became the president. What will be of significance is what difference your life made to those around you. How tall are you standing? As Dr David Molapo asks, 'Are you leaving a legacy or are you leaving a vacancy?'

Ask God to help you to get your priorities right to gain perspective on why you are alive. Let your life move from merely managing frenetic tasks to powerful purposeful living. Ask God to help you to be motivated enough to change the way you use your time, your talents and your treasures. Live with purpose, passion and greater levels of productivity; no longer with powerless pie-in-the-sky planning, pity or pining for what could be.

'But regarding anything beyond this, dear friend, go easy.
There's no end to the publishing of books, and constant study
wears you out so you're no good for anything else. The last
and final word is this: Fear God. Do what He tells you.'
(ECCLESIASTES 12:13)

My Reflections on My Life

◈ So what needs to change – the way you manage your time, your talents, your treasures?

◈ What do you need to let go of to move on to significance?

◈ What is embedded on the inside of you that needs to surface and come to the fore to make a difference to this world?

Making the Most of the Seasons of Your Life ❧

'WHEN WE ARE TRANSFORMED BY CHANGE, OUR LIVES, OUR ACTIONS AND OUR ATTITUDES INVITE OTHERS TO JOIN US. BECAUSE WE ARE CHANGED, WE ARE THEN ABLE TO CHANGE THE WORLD. AND SUDDENLY CHANGE BEGINS TO HAPPEN, NOT ONLY IN US, BUT ALSO BECAUSE OF US. AND THAT IS THE GREATEST MIRACLE OF ALL.'
DALE HANSON BOURKE

It will benefit us to learn to make use of the different seasons in our lives. Every season has a reason and a purpose. As each winter passes, it is a sign for us to come out of hibernation, to put all negativity and disempowering memories behind us, and as the sunflower looks towards the sun, so we need to arise and face the beauty and opportunity that the season ahead has in store. The winter seasons of life are often associated with times of darkness and the cold realities that press in all around. It can also hold a chilling fear of the future that comes in the absence of faith. As nothing can flourish and bloom in a constant state of winter, so without a change of season in our lives, our beauty and potential for progressing into a new growth phase would soon be marred. The changing of the seasons should be an encouraging reminder that no one season lasts forever. Change is one of life's constants. Change grants us the privilege to start all over again.

> The Heavenly Gardener is never so near the vine as when He is pruning it.

There is a wonderful invitation in God's Book for all of us. This invitation is to embrace His abundant life, to be every bit the person He designed us to be, and to be empowered and influential in our unique environments, at home and at work. It is always the season to be gentle and loving and yet at the same time, powerfully purposeful and effective. It is indeed time to turn over a new leaf. We must love being the person we were created to be. Capitalize on the miraculous way God has designed you in spirit, soul and body. Let the beauty of your creation shine through in all that you do! Seasons change. Change happens. Transition phases can be painful. Just as the rose bushes in my delightful garden need to be pruned to the base in order to produce profuse colours and generous blooms, so the process of change must cut deep into our lives in order to produce a harvest of plentiful and good things.

'Blessed is the man
who does not walk in the counsel of the wicked
or stand in the way of sinners
or sit in the seat of mockers.

But his delight is in the law of the LORD,
and on his law he meditates day and night.

He is like a tree planted by streams of water,
which yields its fruit in season
and whose leaf does not wither.
Whatever he does prospers.'
(PSALMS 1:1–3)

The changing seasons in our lives afford us the opportunity to take time to reflect. Just about everyone you speak to these days talks about how there never seems to be enough time to do the things they would like to do, or to accomplish certain goals within defined time frames, not to mention to nurture their all-important relationships. And yet, most often, the change that a new season brings is to get our attention to embrace the current season and not resist it; to turn our face into the wind and allow all the grit and grime that tries to glue us into one space and place to be swept away. The change of seasons is designed to lead us into a time of new beginnings, through an open door and over the threshold to fabulous, limitless opportunities.

The changing of seasons in our lives cannot be ignored. We ignore them to our peril. These changes relentlessly pursue us from our time of birth until the time we depart this earth. Just contemplate for a moment, if you will, the seasons of celebration, of grief, of joy, of hope, of extreme excitement and bitter disappointment as the season of the birth of a child enters our world. Bliss over the 'planned' baby; fear, heartache and disappointment over the baby supposedly out of its season. We choose the outcome, always. Are we bitter or better as we emerge from each season? Changes in family relationships can create summer, winter, autumn and spring seemingly in one go! Engagements, marriage, divorce, the empty nest, and parents entering a nursing home or dying, all bring with them seasons of change. Our seasons of health and the different stages of life can so easily decide for us in a moment whether we are looking at the sun or at the clouds. Changes in career or geographical location are often a bitter-sweet experience. The changing seasons will always be a part of our lives but as someone once said, 'The sun is always shining.' It just depends on how we choose to view the seasons of our lives. Are they bright and light or doom and gloom?

In her book *Quiet Places*, Jane Rubietta wrote on the subject of change: *'If change is inevitable, why waste energy bucking it? Will we allow change to change us for the better? Or will we dig in our heels, leaving skid marks all the way? Surviving change cannot, must not be our only goal. Every event is designed to lead us toward God.'*

There are no guarantees in life, but there is always hope. The hope lies in the seed of potential found in the process of change if we will yield to it and do not circumvent the process. Remembering that the giant oak was once a tiny acorn should be an encouragement to us never to despise the days of small beginnings, but rather to make the most of every season, every moment of our lives so that we never limit ourselves and fall short of aspiring to the greatness that resides within. Put your roots down in the rich soil of faith and water them with joy.

My Reflections on the Changing Seasons in My Life

Gratitude ✎

GRATITUDE IS AN ATTITUDE. GRATITUDE IS A CHOICE. GRATITUDE IS ONE OF THE SECRETS OF CONTENTMENT!

Contentment is recognizing the sacred in the ordinary. We recognize the sacred when we take a moment to give thanks for the wonders in our lives we so often take for granted. The cooling breeze on a blistering hot day. The sticky kiss from your toddler's lips. The reassurance and warmth of your husband's hand at your back. The plate of food full of variety, colour and nutrients designed to keep us healthy. Gratitude is in every one of us. Gratitude is a God-trait but only some people choose to make use of it and enjoy the benefits of a grateful heart.

Being grateful is easy when life is sunshine and roses. It is when it is dark and gloomy that having an attitude of gratitude fades. In times of difficulty, it is important to practise gratitude as much as possible. This is the time, says Kenneth Copeland, when *'Thanksgiving becomes the big gun in our spiritual arsenal. It keeps us connected to God and receiving from Him. Bring the cannon of thanksgiving onto the battlefield of faith.'* Giving thanks and being grateful for each day builds into you a great expectation, as if something wonderful is going to happen. Every day becomes alive with possibilities. You cannot control what is outside of you, but you do have full responsibility for what takes place on the inside of you. Make a quality choice today to rise up in thanksgiving, in praise, with gratitude. Your life may never be the same again. This moment is all you have. Make the most of it. Gratitude is totally within your reach. Gratitude is a choice. You are always only one decision away from changing your perspective, because truth be told, the world is not really the way it is, but it is the way you see it. Just imagine if you started seeing your life and your circumstances through the eyes of gratitude. Gratitude can replace bitterness with sweetness. What has happened has happened and no amount of regretting is going to change that, but gratitude can give you reward in place of regret.

Gratitude expressed is rejoicing in the Lord for Who He is and for the great things He has done. Paul tells us in his letter to the Philippians to *'Rejoice in the Lord always. I will say it again: Rejoice! Let your gentleness be evident to all. The Lord is near. Do not be anxious about anything, but in everything, by prayer and petition, with THANKSGIVING, present your requests to God. And the peace of God, which transcends all understanding, will guard your hearts and minds in Christ Jesus.'* (Philippians 4:4–7). Joy is gratitude for life.

> *A candle loses nothing of its light by lighting another candle.*
>
> JAMES KELLER

On an Oprah Winfrey show, Oprah had a guest who spoke about the value of keeping a Gratitude Diary. Oprah mentioned that she had been keeping a gratitude diary for years and enthused over the many positive changes this had brought about in her life. Can you imagine one of the world's billionaires, a woman with so much political sway keeping a gratitude diary? And yet every day Oprah finds five new things she can be grateful for. What a witness to us of the value of such a daily discipline. Keeping a gratitude diary keeps you living in the moment. It keeps your heart light and thankful. It truly helps you to count those blessings.

Paul goes on to say in Philippians 4:8, *'Finally brothers, whatever is true, whatever is noble, whatever is right, whatever is pure, whatever is lovely, whatever is admirable – if anything is excellent or praiseworthy – think about such things.* Finally, says Paul in verse 11, *For I have learned to be content whatever the circumstances.* This is the true essence of gratitude. Before you sleep, thank God for another day of life. Rest – knowing you are loved, you are blessed, you are held tenderly in the hands of a loving God. Tomorrow is a brand new day to start all over again.

> *'If you concentrate on finding whatever is good in every situation, you will discover that your life will suddenly be filled with gratitude; a feeling that nurtures the soul.'*
>
> RABBI HAROLD KUSHNER

My Reflections on Having an Attitude of Gratitude

Developing Excellence in Your Life ✍

WHAT IS EXCELLENCE? EXCELLENCE IS NOT INBORN. IT IS A CHOICE THAT DETERMINES WHETHER WE LIVE A LIFE OF MEDIOCRITY OR MAGNIFICENCE.

In our high-tech era where stress takes its toll with the ever-increasing demands that are continually made on our time and on our relationships, the pursuit of excellence becomes lost in the fray. This is evidenced in our world by the lack of good customer service, by people not delivering what they promise, by the divorce courts breaking all records in the dismantling of marriages, and it is seen in the complexities of our lives riddled by guilt because we have compromised our own standards. Excellence in life and in business has become a memory.

Excellence is not a virtue we are born with but it is a conscious choice we must make that will bring us a different result in our lives. As Stephen Covey says, if we keep on doing the same old thing, we are going to keep getting the same old results. It is time for us to make a change and pursue excellence. Excellence consistently applied gives you great and well-deserved outcomes.

In the Bible we read the story of Daniel in whom was found an **excellent spirit**. The dictionary defines excellence as possessing an outstanding merit or quality. Because Daniel chose excellence in every area of his life, God granted him a keen mind, knowledge and understanding, and the ability to interpret spiritual concepts and solve difficult problems. In essence, making excellence the pattern of your life means that whatever you think, say and

> *We sow a thought and reap an act. We sow an act and reap a habit. We sow a habit and reap a character. We sow a character and reap a destiny. Excellence therefore is not an act, but must become a way of life.*
>
> WILLIAM THACKERAY

act upon, God can abundantly bless. Excellence never entertains compromise, shoddy workmanship or sloppy attitudes.

Instead of worrying about what people will say of you, why not spend your time trying to accomplish something they will admire you for – a life of excellence.

Excellence is embracing the perception that we belong to the King. We are His Ambassadors, representing Him in everything we are and in everything we do. We may not be perfect, but our hearts and minds are always aiming for excellence.

Perfectionism is often misconstrued as excellence. Perfection belongs to God alone. This was a statement made by the actor Michael J. Fox as he chose to stand tall in the midst of crippling mental and physical health. We can never hope to be perfect in this imperfect world. When we strive for perfectionism at all costs, we destroy any hope of being excellent in anything. Inflexible perfectionism is an issue of control and it makes one critical, harsh and demanding because the standards are so high that in the perfectionist's opinion, no one can ever do it right. The perfectionist's approach then becomes, 'I do it all, because I do it right.' Excellence, however, says, 'I live in an imperfect world with imperfect people, but whatever I do, I do to the best of my ability and even if things don't work out the way I would like, I know I did it with excellence.' The excellent approach to life brings one peace, contentment and less stress.

Every day is an opportunity to choose excellence – to choose His Way, to choose the higher Way. God is excellence because God is Love. Paul says in Corinthians that he will show us a more excellent way and that excellent way is love. If we do everything as unto God and in love, how can we but operate in excellence? It really is the foundational teaching of Jesus... love one another – in word and in deed. Excellence then essentially begins with ordering your internal world and loving yourself as God loves you. You cannot give to someone what you do not have. How much of God's love have you accepted and received for yourself? Personal excellence, then, is gaining the right perception of who you are. Seeing your life through God's eyes means you have no regrets.

Choose today to live the more excellent way – His Way. **Standing tall** in this falling world is going to require excellence over perfection; flexibility over rigidity and peace over panic that is created by trying to live in perfection. Perfectionism is a relationship destroyer and can cause your world to come tumbling down. Excellence, however, is the mainstay and it will be one of the catalysts to open doors of opportunity for you.

My Reflections on Living with Excellence

✧ What are the areas in which you find yourself pursuing perfection?

✧ What has being a perfectionist cost you?

✧ Start today to exchange perfectionism for excellence and live in freedom as you experience the difference.

Alive with Possibility

Possibilities; endless, fathomless, boundless. Yet people seem determined to live under their self-imposed limitations, rather than reach out for the opportunities that are just waiting to be grasped. Many of the circumstances that seemingly interrupt or cause confusion in your day-to-day living are often linked with assumptions that have been created from your past experiences and environmental conditioning in your life. You cannot confidently reach out to the wonderment of possibilities when you are weighed down with bitterness, anxiety, anger and hopelessness. Being alive to every possibility demands that you live in the present moment. Being alive with possibility calls for you to be aware of and be alert enough to catch the eye of the next possibility waiting for you to reach out and take it. Making the most of an opportunity requires your flexibility and letting go of resistance so that you embrace the possibility and do not create impossibility in your mind by making excuses, or talking yourself out of it and derailing yourself before you even start. The possible becomes seemingly impossible when you start speaking negatively and you find reasons why you cannot pursue something or make up your mind that it is not for you before you even begin to explore the abundant potential contained in that opportunity. When your focus is on what you can't do you instantly cut off the creative flow that is required to expand on the possibility. It is like taking an axe to the root of a magnificent rose bush and cutting out any possibility of the rose bush becoming what it was created to be.

One of the best things for a sluggish mind is to disturb its routine.

'One of the best things for a sluggish mind is to disturb its routine', said someone who understands the necessity of the mind being open to possibility. Routine keeps you from taking advantage of the many possibilities that come your way each day. Routine and drudge make you look at an opportunity as just another thing that is going to put more pressure on your time. Circumstances do colour life, but we have the choice of what the colour is going to be. Start today to colour your world with brighter colours that stimulate you and appeal to you. Start to increase your levels of self-worth and appreciate yourself more each day knowing that opportunity is drawn to confidence. Value yourself – you are one of a kind. If you don't make use of the possibilities that come your way, who will? Take your confidence to new heights. Refuse to be intimidated, distracted or disillusioned about what you think you are not capable of achieving. If you achieved all you are capable of, you would be more astounded than anyone else. Release your creativity and inspire others to do the same. Take the cap off your 'inner fragrance bottle' and release the scent for others to enjoy.

> *The future belongs to those who believe in the beauty of their dream.*
>
> ELEANOR ROOSEVELT

Make a choice to live in the power of inspired imagination, not in the past or out of your negative memory bank. When your memories are stronger than your dreams, you are living your life facing backwards! John Maxwell has an extraordinary quotation and it is really worth adopting it for your life: *'He who sees the invisible can achieve the impossible.'*

Be alive with possibility!

My Reflections on Being Alive with Possibility

✧ Make a list of the possibilities that present themselves to you each day.

✧ Find creative ways of making the most of these possibilities.

✧ Possibilities don't always come in the form of a new job offer or new earning potential but often in the form of a thought, an idea, a new of way of thinking and of being. Write them down!

Life is a Little Like Golf 🦋

'**THEY SAY GOLF IS LIKE LIFE, BUT DON'T BELIEVE THEM. GOLF IS MORE COMPLICATED THAN THAT.**'
GARDNER DICKINSON

Life is a little like golf. Early in 2007 my husband gave me the gift of a series of golf lessons with a professional, laughing hysterically at the thought that someone like me – who couldn't kick, catch or hit a ball even with the greatest of focus – would be taking golf lessons with a pro! Little did I know that golf would be one of the vehicles that God would use to teach me a whole lot about the way we should go about our daily lives. I was about to find out that life indeed is a little like golf.

> 'To me, life is like the back nine in Golf. Sometimes you play better on the back nine. You may not be stronger, but hopefully you're wiser. And if you keep most of your marbles intact, you can add a note of wisdom to the coming generation.'
>
> CLINT EASTWOOD

Lesson #1
Don't let your thoughts cause you to abdicate before you have the chance to celebrate!

The worst club in my bag is my brain.
CHRIS PERRY

Standing on the practice mat, looking the part but certainly not feeling it, holding the club awkwardly and nervously and hearing the pro say, 'No pressure, but just hit a couple of balls for me...' No pressure? I couldn't hit a soccer ball with the club, never mind a 4cm ball a metre away from me! 'Dear Lord, what have I got myself into? Why don't I just quit while I am ahead? Whose idea was this anyway? Why didn't I give the gift to someone else who really wants to play golf ?' As I hacked away, missed the ball, scuffed the club, and embarrassed myself, my self-talk really kicked up a notch. 'You will never hit this ball. This is an impossible game. How ridiculous to try to hit such a little ball with such a little piece of iron. This is useless. I am useless!' (Talk about downward spiral talk. Left unchecked, it sure takes its toll). I was ready to abdicate. The pro wasn't. As I adjusted my attitude with great difficulty, I have to say, I was then in a position to humble myself to the process of being taught.

The best wood in most amateurs' bags is the pencil.

AUTHOR UNKNOWN

Pride never learns anything from anyone. We have to put away our pride and open ourselves wide to what can be learnt from someone who has walked the road ahead of us. Our thoughts can derail us before we have even taken our first swing at life! Don't let your thoughts cause you to abdicate before you have the chance to celebrate!

One lesson down, eleven to go with my pro! The second lesson saw me a little more determined to make a better connection with the ball. The secret is that I had to apply what I was being taught, otherwise it was mere information. Any information that we receive must translate into application. I diligently and persistently put into practice what I had learned.

*Lesson #2
Diligence and persistence pay off.*

Persistence fights off procrastination. The more persistent I was, the less I procrastinated, the more confident I became. From the swing, to the short game of pitching and then onto putting made me realize why one world-class golfer said, 'You swing for show, but putt for dough!' Often when you are closest to the hole, or to your target, the easier you think the shot will be. But it is when you are closer to your target that it takes even more diligent application, focus, concentration and determination to 'sink your putt'. What are you focusing on that requires diligence and persistence? Don't give up – be more determined than ever! Do whatever it takes to sink your 'putt'.

> *Lesson #3*
> *Keep your*
> *eye on the ball*
> *and keep your*
> *head down!*

Your 'putt' may be a dream, a decision, a new direction. Aim carefully.

If I heard those words once, I heard them a thousand times. It is nearly impossible to aim for something if you are not looking at it. With golf, as with life, you need eagle-eye vision to ensure that you meet your goal every time. Lifting your head takes your eye away from your goal and the reason we lift our head is because we want to see how far the ball is going to travel and where it is going to land. The result then is we either miss the ball altogether, hit on top of the ball or the ball dribbles about 30cm away from where we are standing. Be sure that you stay focused on the goals you have in your life, and avoid trying to see what the outcome will be before its time. Be faithful doing what you are doing in the moment. Do everything with excellence and with persistence. The result you desire, and more, will soon be yours. The scorecard of your life will start reflecting desires met. Be in the moment and the moment will work for you. Keep your eye on your goal!

The reason the
pro tells you
to keep your
head down is
so you can't see
him laughing!
PHYLLIS DILLER

'There are two things you can do with your
head down – play golf and pray.'
LEE TREVINO

At last the day had arrived that I would emerge from the practice range to the majestic golf course. Feeling a little nervous and intimated at the sheer distance from tee box to the red flag 472 metres away, I could nonetheless feel the surge of excitement that I was on that day accomplishing a deeply hidden desire. What impressed me more than the fact that I was actually playing a game of golf, was the beauty, the sights, the sounds and the quietness that surrounded me. It got me thinking of how often we are so intent on getting our ball in life to the red flag that we forget to stop; to breathe and to recognize and be thankful for our surroundings. Just take a moment out of each hour in your day and acknowledge where you find yourself. You may even be in heavy traffic, but if you stopped being so consumed by what you are doing, you might find a hardy little daisy pushing its way through on the sidewalk to peek at the sun. Find your bright

> *Lesson #4*
> *Take in the sights and the sounds.*

yellow daisy in the busyness of your day. Find that moment, quiet yourself and be still and filled with gratitude knowing that all things have been created for your pleasure.

Yes, yes, and yes again. Your attitude will absolutely determine how well you do in the game of golf and in the more serious game of life. There will be many times you will 'duff the ball', and many times you will have the opportunity to choose your attitude. Once you lose your grip on a good attitude, you lose your grip on the game, on your relationships and on your life. Your attitude determines your direction. Which way are you going? A consistently good attitude is the difference between having just a good game and having a brilliant game. Your consistently bright attitude is going to be the determining factor of the outcome. If it doesn't take much to get you to lose your cool, I would venture to say the game of golf is not for you, and that life might be a little like golf for you… trying, frustrating, and totally demanding! Make it your decision today to change your attitude about the way you play the game of life. At the end of it all, it is not so much whether you won or lost, but how you played the game. Enjoy it!

> *It is almost impossible to remember how tragic a place this world is when one is playing golf.*
> ROBERT LYND

> *Lesson #5*
> *Attitude and consistency are the way to win the game.*

'If you wish to hide your character, do not play golf.'
PERCY BOOMER

*'The only time my prayers are never
answered is on the golf course.'*
BILLY GRAHAM

'May thy ball lie in green pastures... and not in still waters.'
AUTHOR UNKNOWN

My Reflections on the Game of Life

✧ Have you found yourself taking life so seriously that you cannot enjoy it?

✧ What applications from the analogy of life being a little like golf can you take and apply to your own life?

Attitude is Life – Life is Attitude 🌹

Your attitude is one of your most influential possessions in your life. It is one of the master keys to open the doors of peace, joy, achievement and fulfilment in your life. The outworking of your life is undoubtedly linked to your attitude towards your life. Having the right attitude is like having the right combination for the safe of your life. A safe holds prized and precious possessions; things of great importance are kept in a safe. When you are able to open the safe of your life with the right attitude, there is no limit to the powerful treasures you can access. It is your attitude at the beginning of your day, at the start of a task, at the commencement of a new job, in the midst of your trials, in the complexity of your relationships and in the challenge of a new opportunity that determines how effective you will be in securing a beneficial outcome. It is choosing to have the right attitude before you start that can mean the difference between success and failure. It is your attitude that will determine your experience. We have all heard the saying, 'Life is what you make it.' I would like to add to that: 'Your attitude will determine what you make of life.'

> *My mind is my biggest asset. I expect to win every tournament I play.*
>
> TIGER WOODS

It is indeed your attitude towards life which will determine life's attitude towards you. What you put out there will come back to you. What you sow in your attitudes will be what you reap in the attitudes of others. Your attitude is dictated by you alone. No one else can take the blame for your attitude today. Life is attitude. You control your attitude 24/7. If you decide to adopt a negative, gloomy attitude, life will be negative and gloomy. If you decide to adopt a positive attitude in a negative circumstance, you may well be surprised! The negative circumstance may not instantly resolve but will be much more bearable because of your approach and mindset towards it. You cannot rectify a negative situation with a negative attitude. Negative on negative repels! Opposites attract! Convert your negatives to a positive. Develop a foundational attitude which accepts there is more in you that is designed to succeed than to fail.

Even if you don't 'feel positive' about something, act as if you do. Live in it, even though it may not be your current reality. A good attitude is a matter of choice, not a matter of feeling or circumstance. Actions trigger feelings. Harness a great attitude, and let the rewards of that choice follow and live with the feelings you have created, and not what is dictated to you. What you focus on has your attention. Focus on what you want to experience in your life and see yourself being successful in what you put your hand and mind to. Autograph your life with excellence. Think, walk, live, act and conduct yourself in a manner that leads you to the place you desire to be. Having a fabulous attitude is catchy. People want to be around someone who is confident and light-hearted, and someone who is solution-minded and joyful. When this is your attitude, you can easily treat everybody as if they are the most important person in the world. Now this is really a key to opening that safe to the great and worthy possessions of your life.

Attitudes are often based on assumptions. To assume, as a person so humorously said, 'makes an ass out of you and me!' (ass/u/me) Assumption-based attitudes can be traced to how you see or feel about yourself. If you walk into a room and suddenly people start talking in a whisper or perhaps laugh at something, you can instantly assume that they are talking or laughing about you. This will undoubtedly affect

A great flame follows a little spark.

DANTE ALIGHIERI

your attitude for the rest of the occasion. For this attitude to change, you must change. How do you change? You change by trading your assumptions for fact! What are the facts that can affect your attitude to life?

1. You are created by God.

2. God loves you more than you can comprehend.

3. God sent His Son Jesus to give you life in abundance.

4. You can be confident because in Jesus all your sins are forgiven – forever. No more guilt!

5. Everything you need pertaining to life is yours, if you will just receive it.

6. The only person whose opinion really counts is God.

7. You can walk into a room with confidence, like you own it, because you are owned by God!

Your life is so special that you owe it to yourself to have the right attitude to life.

Get His attitude for life – because you're worth it.

'When your attitude is right, there is no barrier too high, no valley too deep, no dream too extreme, no challenge too great for you.'

CHARLES SWINDOLL

My Reflections on My Attitude

✧ Make a quality decision today to put the axe to the root of all ungodly attitudes that keep tripping you up and robbing from your life.

✧ Make a list of all the attitudes that drive your life and make a decision to make the exchange. His attitudes for yours!

The Time of Your Life ✎

WHAT YOU DO TODAY, YOU WILL LIVE THROUGH TOMORROW.

Time is the one equalizing factor of all mankind. Everyone has the same amount of time allocated to them. It is what we do with time that decides whether we master it or we become enslaved to it. One of the most important numbers you will ever learn in your life is the number 1440. This number is the number of minutes that make up your 24-hour day. It is the number that determines your productivity and effectiveness in each given day. John Maxwell, the well-known writer and speaker on human behaviour and leadership, has said that if he came home with you today and spent 24 hours with you, he would be able to tell you within 99.9% accuracy how successful your day-to-day life will be. He will do this simply by looking at the way you plan to spend your daily allocation of 24 hours. It's a concept really worth thinking about, since, love it or leave it, time rules our lives. It is a fantasy to believe you can control and manage time. You can, however, control and manage yourself. Time is seemingly so difficult to define and often like a slippery bar of soap; it doesn't matter how tightly we try to hold onto it, it just keeps slipping away. Yet without doubt we can acknowledge that if we do not master our lives within the time we have been allocated, we will become its slave!

1440 is one of the most important numbers of your life. These are the minutes that make up your 24-hour day. What are you doing with your 1440 minutes?

Time means a variety of things to so many different people. To your baby, time is based on the need to be fed, on nappy changes, or having more sleep. A toddler believes he can keep up the activity 28 hours a day and it is still not enough. To a school student, the time for school and studying cannot pass quickly enough. The weeks go too slowly and the weekends are way too fast. To those in love, time seemingly does not exist as long as they can be with the one they love. The mother tending her young ones wishes there was a way to extend the night hours so she can get the sleep she craves, and deserves. For the businessman or woman, time means reaching deadlines, meeting the constant daily demands of running a business, and perhaps travelling around the world; sometimes with time and sometimes against time. Traffic delays can mean a waste of time. It doesn't have to be, though, if you use that time wisely and add value to your life by listening to something inspirational, uplifting and meaningful, instead of fuming in the traffic fumes. To the retired woman, time is a gift to spend with her grandchildren, time that perhaps she could never spend with her own children. Time, you see, is not really what it is. It is what you make of it.

> *Spend time with those you love. One of these days you will either say, 'I wish I had,' or 'I'm glad I did.'*
>
> ZIG ZIGLAR

Time is something you need to make work for you and not let it work against you. Don't abuse time and set yourself up for failure. When you are enslaved to time, that is the call to retreat. Step back, refocus, readjust and redress your life so you can advance to face the time-snatching stressors in your life.

> *'Busyness rapes relationships. It substitutes shallow frenzy for deep friendships. It promises satisfying dreams, but delivers hollow nightmares. It feeds the ego, but starves the inner man. It fills the calendar, but fractures the family. It cultivates a programme, but replaces important priorities.'*
>
> AUTHOR UNKNOWN

Unbridled busyness can relentlessly invade our lives. Just a few decades ago business decisions would take months to formulate as documents travelled to and fro by boat and then by plane. Today we face compression of time, especially since new and faster technology is developed by the hour. It now takes mere seconds to receive a communication via email, or to do a transaction over the internet. Uninterrupted time is required to formulate a meaningful response. Responding under pressure to important requests can cause even greater pressure if it delivers undesirable results. Not doing it right the first time around means that you have to find more time to get it right a second time. Doing it right today means no regrets tomorrow.

Practise the habit of living in the moment!

So how do you make time an ally and not an enemy? **Standing tall** when time is running out requires that we practise the habit of living in the moment. I say practise the habit, because living in the moment needs to become a way of life and will only become so when it is practised. Practising the habit is a process of re-conditioning your life. Habits do not change overnight and if you have been in the habit of worrying or living with tomorrow's load today, that habit will need to be relentlessly worked on. One of the major reasons that we are in dis-ease or are diseased is because we endeavour to carry yesterday's baggage into an already busy today and worry about what may happen tomorrow. Today, this moment in time, is your only reality. Maximize this moment – it is the only one you have. Make this moment in time count for you. Live in the present and give your undivided attention to what you are doing right now. Let your mind and body occupy the same space at the same time. When you are driving your car, focus on driving your car. When your teenager comes and curls up on the couch next to you to connect with you, switch off the TV or put your magazine or newspaper down and be in that moment of connectivity. When you are at your place of work, be at your place of work. There is nothing like missing the moment to breed regret. Often the moment is missed because your thoughts are elsewhere. The Greek word for worry is *merimnao* which, directly translated, means to be distracted, fragmented and full of anxiety! Don't store up today's tasks for tomorrow, otherwise you are already compressing tomorrow before it is even here and that will, once again, make you feel enslaved to time. Resist inflexibility to changing circumstances. Inflexibility will cause you to snap like a reed. Flexibility is required to work with the times and changing seasons of your life.

Not everything will always work out the way you would like it to, but knowing that you can accommodate change will cause you to embrace the change and your time will be lived with a more positive frame of mind. Don't allow unresolved issues to remain that way. Dragging around unresolved issues with you day after day

Eternity was in that moment.

WILLIAM CONGREVE

is bound to impact negatively not only your time, but your energy and output levels. Today is the day to be free of everything that would hold you back from having the best times of your life. Be thankful, grateful and content. So much more could go wrong with your life; however, when you look at how much has gone right in your life, how much is going right in your life and how much you have been blessed with, thankfulness should become a way of life.

'Why some go on to success and others don't is not a mystery – the key is discipline. Discipline is the willingness to do what you know you should do even when you don't feel like it.'

ROB RUFUS

My Reflections on Having the Time of My Life

❖ How are you filling the minutes of your days? Remember minutes soon become hours, then days, then months, then years! Be sure not to find regret at the end.

❖ Stop for a moment and give thanks to God for the wonderment of your life. Gratitude makes way to receive even greater blessing.

Finding the Balance in Life ✍

'YOU ALWAYS DO WHAT YOU WANT TO DO. THIS IS TRUE WITH EVERY ACT. YOU MAY SAY THAT YOU HAD TO DO SOMETHING, OR THAT YOU WERE FORCED TO, BUT ACTUALLY WHATEVER YOU DO, YOU DO BY CHOICE. ONLY YOU HAVE THE POWER TO CHOOSE FOR YOURSELF.'
W. CLEMENT STONE

Many people often put their lives on hold in the pursuit of achieving success in one particular area, i.e. career, sport, stardom, only to feel dissatisfied when they reach their perceived destination.

This reality is observed when a career endeavour becomes all-consuming and is at the cost of family, fun, good health and freedom. There are times and seasons in one's career when a greater investment must be made. However, balance is always the key to greater effectiveness. If you allow yourself to live your life in the equilibrium that stems from having an ordered life, you have far greater resources from which to draw to nurture great relationships, be satisfied in your work, and anything else that is important to you. If the balance is weighed down with the extremes of overwork and the neglect of that which is valuable to you, soon just the sheer fatigue and feelings of compromise and even guilt can cause you to be much less effective in your daily activities.

> *Opportunity is missed by most people because it is dressed in overalls and looks like work.*
>
> THOMAS EDISON

Work-Life Balance is achieved when you manage yourself and your responsibilities with discipline and when the Ladder of your Life is stepped in order of priority. The Ladder of your Life is created when you take the time to decide what is most important in your life and work it down to what is the least important. The least important shouldn't feature much on your radar screen but the most important down to midway important should have your attention. The balance becomes evidenced when your time, attention and resources are averaged over your priorities from the most important to the least important. Creating this balance will require flexibility and adaptability as demands vary, and change remains a constant in your life.

Blessed are the balanced for they shall outlast everyone!

As you keep your focus aligned with your priorities, manage stress levels and commit yourself to constant personal transformation, your days will become more ordered, and your relationships will be given the quality and quantity of time they deserve. You will begin to reap the rewards of investing your time, talent and treasures wisely and achieving work-life balance will become a way of life for you.

Areas of priority which you will need to take into consideration are:

- Your Personal Life – What has heart and meaning for you?

- Your Spiritual Life

- Your Spouse or Partner

- Your Children

- Your extended Family

- Your mental, emotional and physical life

- Your Career and your responsibilities

- Your Personal Goals

- Your Personal growth and development plan

- Your Financial situation

- Leisure and Travel

- Social, Hobbies and Interests

The search for, and making the adjustments to find, the balance in your life, will require you to remember that it is not the mountain ahead that wears you out, *it is the grain of sand in your shoe!*

There is an unfailing, unchanging principle in life and that is what you sow you will reap and where you sow is going to be the area from which you reap. Your reward will return to you from the area where you make the biggest investment of your time, your treasures and your talents. The key is to try to find the balance between your personal life, your personal relationships and your career. Where would you most like to reap the reward?

Finding the balance can create a whirlwind in our lives because there always seem to be a hundred-and-one reasons why we should be spending more time at the office or socializing, and we could be neglecting those areas we take for granted, such as the people in our lives.

There are many self-imposed obstacles that come into play in finding the balance in your life. I have highlighted just a few:

1. **Perfectionism:** Your attitude to your responsibilities at work or in the home is, 'I do it all, because I do it right.' Your workload goes out of whack and if you are in a management position, you rob others of the opportunity to take responsibility and to grow in their position. If you are doing all the work at home, you will eventually become resentful with everyone in the home because it will feel like you are doing all the work and nobody else supports your perfectionist mindset and actions.

2. **Routine:** Drudge and routine keep you from flexing, taking time out and creating space to ponder the big picture. Routine keeps you in your comfort zone and stifles creativity. Routine also makes you grumpy because you begin to experience life as lacklustre and boring. Routine should be rooted out of your life and you should endeavour to find new and creative ways of doing the same things – the things that need to be done.

3. **Being constantly busy:** The root of this is often low self-esteem and therefore the mindset of 'If I'm busy I must be valuable' holds you captive. Being busy is not necessarily always productive. Being

effective is. Being busy will make you exhausted, and you will feel unappreciated because it seems that no one else is running at your pace. Busy does not equate to effectiveness. Perhaps it is time to check out what is keeping you so busy and ask yourself if it is really worth it. What is your payoff? How effective could you be if you cut down even a quarter of the 'stuff ' you are busy with?

People who live effective and calmly productive lives, those who live in the wisdom of balance being the key to life, have very distinct evidence of the following qualities in their lives:

- They are calm, confident and clear-minded and not easily flustered.

- Their relationships at home and at work are enjoyable, comfortable and respectable.

- These people are really positive, enthusiastic and future-minded.

- They are able to inspire others to find the balance in their lives.

- They live ordered lives and take full responsibility for their outcomes.

Time is the best-kept secret of the rich! This is a fact. Time is more valuable than money. You can make more money but not more time! Learn to say no in the nicest possible way. Don't let your mouth overload your back.

*'Just because we increase the speed of information,
does not mean we can increase the speed of decisions.
Pondering, reflecting and ruminating are
undervalued skills in our culture.'*
DALE DAUTEN

'Time is the best-kept secret of the rich.'
RON KUSSMAUL

My Reflections on Finding Balance in My Life

Network to Build Your Net Worth ✺

NETWORKING IS GOD'S IDEA.

Networking is God's idea; it is not a new-generation concept, but a very ancient Biblical concept. Networking is relational, connecting and bridge-building. Networking is the silent-invisible work of the Holy Spirit, accomplishing all that the Father desires so that His Son might be glorified.

> *'What I do believe is that you'll remember those moments*
> *in your life when you were fully involved, fully belonging and*
> *fully appreciated, those moments when you gave yourself*
> *completely to whatever it was you were doing. You will see those*
> *times for what they were – times when you were fully alive!'*
>
> ROBIN SIEGER

One thing I am certain of is that God is building His Kingdom through the many creative, wonderful, committed people in His network, as different as we all may be; He is getting the job done and we are all privileged to be part of this amazing emergence of Christ revealed to the world in and through His Living Body. Networking starts with having a vision and a sense of purpose that is far bigger than something you are able to achieve on your own.

Networking is based on the law of sowing and reaping.

Networking is a skill that is birthed out of having a spirit of generosity, owning a bridge-building mentality and it takes being aware; being present in the moment, being aware of Who is leading and guiding you, of what is on God's heart and what His agenda is, being aware of who you are in Him, and who the people are with whom you interact at any given moment. How do you know that you are not interacting or engaging with someone who could be a significant player in your future? Networking is based on the law of sowing and reaping. If you help others support their God-given dream and vision, God will help you build yours.

> 'You will find, as you look back upon life, that the moments that stand out are the moments when you have done things for others.'
> HENRY DRUMMOND

Great networkers make heart-to-heart connections and build their networks on relationships rather than the returns they will get. Networkers are connection specialists. They see the bigger picture but live their life frame by frame. They see the future but live abundantly in the present. Powerful networkers network ethically, professionally, courteously and with great integrity. As Christians we need to base our networking on the fact that we are representatives of Jesus Christ and of His Kingdom. We are His ambassadors and should reflect Him in every interaction we undertake.

Nigel Risner authored a book called *You Had Me at Hello*. This is how powerful our impact should be on those we meet and network with. Essentially networking is about treating people the way you wish to be treated.

The powerful networker must have an abundance mentality. Often we resist networking and sharing because we are afraid that someone else might steal our ideas. But remember we know a God who owns creativity! He is never in short supply of new ideas, concepts and insights. There are plenty of opportunities for everyone – plenty of ideas, creative imagination and someone else always has what could be of great value to you. What you give out comes back to you, and with God's blessings. If you give out help, you get back help; give out love, you get back love; give out information, you get back information. The challenge, of course, is that although for you the giving is instant, the receiving may not happen in the short term, and often not in the way you would expect it to return to you, or from the

Powerful Networkers must have an abundance mentality.

person you may expect it to come from. Great networkers of faith do believe intrinsically that what they give out will come back a hundredfold. However, don't try to manipulate how it will come back to you. This occurs when you give without an expectation of receiving something. You do something for someone not to get something back, but because you want to help them achieve their goal. It is God's principle and law that you will reap what you have sown. It's not your responsibility to force a return. Always check your motives as to why you are partnering with someone and make sure your motives stay pure.

> *'Keep a sharp eye out for competent men – men who*
> *fear God, men of integrity, men who are incorruptible*
> *– and appoint them as leaders over groups organized*
> *by the thousand, by the hundred, by fifty, and by ten.*
> *They'll be responsible for the everyday work of judging*
> *among the people. They'll bring the hard cases to*
> *you, but in the routine cases they'll be the judges.*
> *They will share your load and that will make it easier*
> *for you. If you handle the work this way, you'll have the*
> *strength to carry out whatever God commands you,*
> *and the people in their settings will flourish also.'*
> (EXODUS 18:17)

A great example of Powerful Networking is part of the life story of Moses. Moses' task of problem-solving for the people of Israel was way beyond his ability to handle, and it was his wise father-in-law who warned him of burn-out if he carried on without networking with others to fulfil the requirement of meeting so many needs.

Moses proved that networking is strongly related to being obedient. We are all standing on the shoulders of other people. Going it alone often means burn-out, discouragement and disillusionment.

Moses learnt about building strategic alliances. Strategic alliances can be described as a coming together of two or more parties who agree to certain behaviours or procedures for the purpose of ultimately creating mutually beneficial results. Strong leaders know that strong alliances will assist them to reach many individuals with whom they may not physically be able to spend time. Strategic alliances are hard work. They are like many of the important relationships in your life; they take time to yield results.

The story of Joseph is a great example of the power that is released through networking. Joseph was a gifted man; a man whose gift made room for him and brought him before great men. Through a series of life-challenging events, Joseph found himself in prison, stripped of his coat, stripped of his dreams, and seemingly stripped of his future, but powerful in using his gift to interpret dreams! Joseph was able to interpret the dreams of the butler and the baker. Little did Joseph know that the butler was to be the bridge-builder, the connection specialist, the networker between himself and the Pharaoh! Joseph was promoted from the pit to the palace and became the second most powerful man in the nation of Egypt. At the same time his people were in famine, but because of Joseph's new position of authority, he was able to feed his brothers and then a nation! Never underestimate the power of networking! Your gift and your connections could well be what brings you before great men and creates a future for many!

> *Most people give up just when they are about to achieve success.*
>
> *They quit on the one-yard line. They give up at the last minute of the game, one foot from a winning touchdown.*
>
> H. ROSS PEROT

We need to network and develop strategic relationships with other like-minded people for the purpose of becoming effective world-changers. Effective Networking is God's trumpet call for us to be part of His global plan to connect people from the four corners of the earth to accomplish His plans. Let us no longer remain divided by our clan, our colour, our cause, our creed or our community. We can no longer remain divided over our diversity. Let's not limit God with our limited thinking. Let us acknowledge that there are many, many parts to the

Body – and how divided we will be if we all act in isolation. Commit to step out of your comfort zone and work on your networking skills – you may never know when you will forge an invaluable strategic alliance!

Tell me and I forget. Show me and I remember.
Involve me and I understand.
CHINESE PROVERB

My Reflections on Networking

❖ How often do I just take for granted the people that I meet instead of looking at them with eyes of 'strategic alliance'?

❖ Never underestimate the need for the right set of connections. Keep your life open to them!

Journey to Your Promised Land 🌿

'FOR THE **LORD** YOUR GOD IS BRINGING YOU INTO A GOOD LAND OF FLOWING STREAMS AND POOLS OF WATER, WITH FOUNTAINS AND SPRINGS THAT GUSH OUT IN THE VALLEYS AND HILLS. IT IS A LAND OF WHEAT AND BARLEY; OF GRAPEVINES, FIG TREES, AND POMEGRANATES; OF OLIVE OIL AND HONEY. IT IS A LAND WHERE FOOD IS PLENTIFUL AND NOTHING IS LACKING. IT IS A LAND WHERE IRON IS AS COMMON AS STONE, AND COPPER IS ABUNDANT IN THE HILLS.'
(DEUTERONOMY 8:7–9)

Every person will at some stage go through the invitational transformation process to get from the wilderness to the Promised Land. The transformation process requires an inside-out approach to shift the obstacles that keep you trapped and hinder your ability to impact your external environment. Transformation means letting go of those things that weigh you down and overwhelm you, so you are able to travel light to the Promised Land that awaits you. The wilderness is a terrible place to live because it is characterized by isolation, rejection, desperation and even devastation. The wilderness is where you live when you don't willingly go through the process of personal transformation.

If you remember that the wilderness is a vital part of the journey, the Promised Land looks far more promising. Emerging out of the wilderness calls for your willingness not to let your past interfere with your present, or dabble with your future. It requires your enthusiasm to live life to the full, to work well, to love unconditionally. You must be aware, be alert and insightful enough to recognize when your Promised Land reveals itself. Be prepared to take risks and to take action. Your life-leadership cannot be built on what you are going to do. Take responsibility for who you are, for your actions, and for your outcomes. The moment you blame-shift, you shift your

> *Nothing is more difficult, and therefore more precious, than to be able to decide.*
>
> NAPOLEON BONAPARTE

responsibility to someone else and diminish your leadership in the eyes of others. Never stop the quest for self-development, improvement, and personal and career growth. You can't inspire others if you stay stuck in the wilderness. You are a real candidate to inspire others when you come out the other side strengthened, renewed, transformed and ready to make a difference to the world around you. You can then share your journey from a position of strength for the benefit of others.

What does your Promised Land look like? Stop for a moment, take a notepad and pen and write down what you experience when you find yourself in the wilderness: lack of provision, weariness, frustration, low-to-no productivity, feelings of uselessness and idleness? This in itself should be the catalyst to make you want to press on very swiftly to your Promised Land. Now write down what your land of Promise holds. What changes do you need to make to transition from the wilderness to the Promised Land? Be encouraged by the words of Barack Obama: *'Change will not come if we wait for some other person or some other time. We are the ones we've been waiting for.'* What price are you prepared to pay to get there? How desperately do you want to be out of the wilderness? What more needs to happen before you make the change?

What is the use of having a vision to conquer the world if you don't have the inner fortitude to conquer yourself?

'Where there is no vision, the people cast off restraint, or perish!'
(PROVERBS 29:18)

You must be able to craft the vision for the way forward. Knowing how to get to this Promised Land is going to require skilful strategic thinking, taking everything and everyone into account. See the bigger picture before you, the new bountiful horizon, and let it become a beacon light for you shining on the direction all the way. Dream it, believe it, see it, tell it, plan it, work it and enjoy it. Just do it!

Enjoy your journey.

My Reflections on My Journey
to the Promised Land

Empowered for Life 🕊

As the saying goes, the journey of 1000 miles begins with a single step. It is also said that the gate of history turns on small hinges. So it is with our lives. It is those small choices and small decisions which all compound to result in the final outcome of your ONE life.

This is ONE LIFE I have been given ~
ONE LIFE filled with purpose and destiny.
This is ONE DAY in my life, created just for me ~
ONE DAY that I can be all I choose to be.
This is ONE MINUTE of my life ~
ONE MINUTE never to be given again.
This ONE SECOND in my life
is part of the MINUTES
that make up my DAYS
which form MY LIFE ~
What am I doing with this ONE LIFE?

To be empowered means to have authority and to have the ability to take action. The empowered person is someone who has a productivity mindset, is curious and abandons the way of thinking that says 'nobody knows and who cares?' An empowered mind learns from others who are successful, and believes there is always a solution to every situation. They are open to new opportunities and find new and creative ways to capitalize on the opportunities. Furthermore they will take the risk to meet the challenge that faces them. Once they have gained knowledge, they apply it and avoid behaviour that doesn't work for them. Empowered people are dependable, reliable and if they say they will do something, they will! Empowered people are in a continual process of transformation and reformation. Transformation means dramatic change! Reformation is working toward the removal of your faults and errors. Reformation takes you closer to your fulfilment.

ONE Choice .... To change, grow and develop

ONE Decision................. To let go of the past

ONE Great Attribute .... Expressed consistently

ONE Empowered .... Positive Attitude

ONE New Realization ..... Of your value and worth

ONE Recognition .... Of how many people your one life influences

ONE Resolution.............. To take responsibility for your one life

ONE Heart Filled .... With an attitude of gratitude

CAN MAKE THE DIFFERENCE BETWEEN
LIVING ONE MEDIOCRE OR ONE MAGNIFICENT LIFE!

Every day you are faced with a choice as to whether you will live an empowered and magnificent life, or a disempowered mediocre life. You are planning for your future today! Every choice you make is going to take you down Magnificent Road or Mediocre Road – there is no middle road. If you don't plan for tomorrow in your choices today, you are going to have to live through it either way! Living an empowered life should be part of your personal constitution. Your personal constitution should define your personal values, your boundaries and morals, your personal and career objectives, and all should be focusing on what you believe your purpose and vision for your life is.

Vision is the image projecting into the future, despite the reality of the current.

KEN BLANCHARD

Never presume on the future and remember that all things in this life are subject to change!

- How empowered am I?

- Does someone else dictate my life?

- What one choice do I need to make in order to change, grow and develop?

- What do I need to let go of in my past so that I can live freely?

- What great attribute do I possess that I know I can express consistently to make a difference to my life?

- What is the one empowered positive attitude I have that works for me?

  _____

  _____

  _____

- What can I recognize today to make me realize my value and my worth?

  _____

  _____

  _____

- Just how many people does my one life influence?

  _____

  _____

  _____

- How can I take full responsibility of my one life today?

  _____

  _____

  _____

- How can my life be filled with an attitude of gratitude?

  _____

  _____

  _____

- What am I thankful for?

  _____

  _____

  _____

Chapter Five

~

Standing Tall In Your Spirit

Spirit – Every human being is made up of a spirit, a soul (which is your mind, your will and your emotions), and a body. Your spirit is who you really are; it is where you communicate with your Creator. It is where you experience the birth of the life you were created to live. Within every human being is a heart-shaped vacuum, designed to be filled by the Presence and love of God alone. People try, by any means, to fill that heart-shaped vacuum using every substitute to fill the void that keeps them wondering why the things of this world never satisfy or meet their needs.

To deny you have a spirit is like trying to live life sitting on a two-legged stool. You are destined to fall before you even get the chance to stand tall. Human beings really are spirit beings having a human experience and not human beings having a spiritual experience.

You were created for wholeness, abundance and to live a fulfilled life. This can only be your reality when you open your life up to the Holy Spirit. The Holy Spirit is the Spirit of God, Who is eternal and has existed forever. The Spirit of God knows all things and is the Source of Power to stand tall, to live victoriously and in the abundance that you were designed to enjoy. He is your Comforter, your Helper, and your greatest and most trusted Partner in life.

When the daily challenges of life close in on you, or you lack direction and need guidance; when you can't find a solution, you can always depend on the Spirit of God to guide you in truth, to lead you by still waters and to restore your soul. With Him you can pass through deep waters and you will not drown, and you need never fear evil, for He will always be with you.

Everyone Needs a Miracle

CAN YOU IMAGINE YOUR SENSE OF FREEDOM AS YOU RECEIVE A NEW LIFE WHERE ALL THE PAIN, THE SIN AND THE GUILT OF YOUR PAST IS NO LONGER BILLED TO YOUR ACCOUNT?

D id you wake up this morning amidst hopelessness and despair, wondering if anything was ever going to change, or if that depression would lift? Perhaps you contemplated the daunting tasks of the day and wished that you could escape not only for today but also for the rest of your life? Surprisingly, despite the success that you may have achieved in your life, you still feel disappointed and disillusioned. You know somehow there must be more. And there is. Everyone needs a miracle and today could be the day that you reach out and receive yours. A miracle that won't just be for today, but one that will last you beyond your lifetime in this falling world. What God wants for you is a brand new life. He wants you to arise and be everything He created you to be. This is not the old life just forgiven, polished up a little, patted on the back with a word of encouragement, and sent out into the world again; this is a brand new life, created for you through the love of Jesus Christ.

Everyone needs a miracle and today could be the day that you reach out and receive yours.

Can you imagine your sense of freedom as you receive this new life and all the pain, the sin and the guilt of the past are no longer billed to your account? What would it be like to wake up tomorrow and experience freedom from the depression and guilt caused by regret and wrongdoing? Imagine the joy as you pull back the curtains and see the beauty of the world with new eyes, no longer dimmed by self-inflicted pain as a result of making crippling choices?

God has made your miracle as simple as believing the ABC.

This new life can be yours right now. No, you don't have to be perfect before you accept God's invitation; none of us would make the grade if that were the case. All you have to do is come just as you are and believe that Jesus came to this earth to wash away your sin with His very own Blood.

It is the perfect exchange: His spotless life given in exchange for your life. Yes, it is a complex concept to grasp; that one sinless Man who actually is God, would choose to take upon Himself the sin of the world because He knew that it would be the only way man could access new life. For when God the Father looks at you, He no longer sees the issues of your past, but He sees you as spotless as He sees His own Son, simply because you have chosen to make the choice to put your faith in His sinless sacrifice to save your life. Complex it is, but so powerful and life-changing when you get it! This was the choice that the Son of God made, to enable you to exercise your power of choice and accept His sacrifice for you. You can try to intellectualize this, you can try to rationalize and analyse His gift to you, but all He requires is that you believe! It sounds too easy I know, but God has made it as simple as believing the A,B,C.

This life of prayer and new-found peace can be yours right now!

'**A**ll have sinned and come short of the Glory of God.'
(ROMANS 3:23)

'**B**ehold the Lamb Who takes away the sin of the world.'
(JOHN 1:29)

'**C**ome to Me all who labour and are heavy laden, and I will give you rest.'
(MATTHEW 11:28)

Prayer is quite simply talking to God. No high-minded language needed, nor do you require permission to approach God. He wants to speak with you more than you want to speak with Him. And even when you don't know how to pray, be encouraged by this:

> 'Meanwhile, the moment we get tired in the waiting, God's Spirit
> is right alongside helping us along. If we don't know how or
> what to pray, it doesn't matter. He does our praying in and for
> us, making prayer out of wordless sighs, our aching groans.'
> (ROMANS 8:26)

His invitation to you today is to be His Guest and receive your personal miracle. I know you don't understand how God, the Creator of the universe and everything in it, would want to speak with you, but He does. I also know that perhaps you don't feel worthy and in fact feel downright uncomfortable with the whole idea. But I have good news for you today. I can testify to the indisputable fact that God has a complete and more fulfilling life for you to live than anything your dreams could have imagined. Whilst you have been dissatisfied and downhearted, He has been knocking at the door of your heart, like a life-insurance salesman, wanting to give you an eternal future and great hope to live each day of your life in joyous fulfilment and contentment. It's true; you do have the freedom to choose anything you want in life… your attitudes, your career, your marriage partner, how you spend your money, and what you do with God's invitation. When God created you He gave you freedom of choice that expresses itself in your free will. He gave you the power to choose, because if mankind was not free to choose, we would not have to be accountable for what we do with our lives and would simply be living like robots. When you stop to think about the huge responsibility you have in exercising your free will, you realize that God took an enormous risk when He imprinted free will into mankind,

God's greatest gift to man is Eternal Salvation that has come to us, graciously free through His Son Jesus Christ. His love is extended towards you today.

because He knew that we could use this powerful weapon even against Him, if we choose to do so.

Everyone needs a miracle. There is no greater miracle than the **NEW BIRTH MIRACLE**. Who among us can truly say, 'I do not need a new life. The old life has been good! I am satisfied to meet my Creator? May we never have to say, 'If only I had my life over again…'

> 'But now the LORD Who created you says, "Do
> not be afraid, for I have ransomed you; I HAVE
> CALLED YOU BY NAME, YOU ARE MINE."'
>
> (ISAIAH 43:1)

> 'Jesus speaking… "You didn't choose me! I chose
> you. I appointed you to go and produce good fruit
> always, so that no matter what you ask for from the
> Father, using My Name, He will give it to you."'
>
> (JOHN 15:16)

When we come to Jesus, He will never again remember our sins… as far as the east is from the west; so far will He remove them from you. (Psalm 103:12). He came to give you life, and life more abundantly. Why spend another day living your old life when right this moment in your life, all things can become new? See your old life in your hands. Hand that old life back to God. There is nothing more you need to do than give your old life to God, receive His new life in you, and make a choice not to return to your old life again. Everybody on earth needs this miracle. Today is your day for a miracle!

Pray this Prayer and Stand Tall in Your New Life!

> Lord, today I give you back my old life, and I thank you for my new
> life in Jesus Christ. I thank you that even though undeserving,
> You love me and You wash away my sins, guilt and pain never to
> remember them again. I turn away from everything in my life that is
> not of You and therefore is not pleasing to You. I thank You for the
> New Birth Miracle that has just taken place in my life. I choose life

and I choose to be in unbroken relationship with You all the days of my life. In the Name of Jesus, my Lord and Saviour, I pray. Amen.

Your new life in Christ is truly the beginning of your real life. God has a plan for your life and a purpose for you to fulfil. You have been created for a reason and His desire is to fulfil that in you, as you become an integral part of His plans for this earth. Be blessed in health, wealth, prosperity and joy, and be empowered by The Holy Spirit. Remember, God is closer to you than your own skin.

My Reflections on My New Birth Miracle

Redeemed to be Free ❧

'IF WE FREELY ADMIT THAT WE HAVE SINNED AND CONFESS OUR SINS, HE IS FAITHFUL AND JUST, TRUE TO HIS OWN NATURE AND PROMISES, AND WILL FORGIVE OUR SINS, DISMISS OUR LAWLESSNESS AND CONTINUOUSLY CLEANSE US FROM ALL UNRIGHTEOUSNESS.'
(1 JOHN 1:9)

The soul consists of your mind, your will and your emotions; three very powerful positive or negative motivating factors in your life. Inner healing and restoration take place in the area of your soul. Your soul is the emotional arena of your life and projects every personal feeling; love, hate, hurt, compassion, happiness, anger, shame and guilt, among others. Your mind holds your thoughts, memories, intellect and imagination. Your personality is a reflection of the condition of your soul. Your soul is the region in which your character is developed and is expressed. Your body is your physical being. It is that part which you and others see, the fleshy or tangible part of your life, and the part which sadly most people focus on to the exclusion of the spirit and the soul. Your body is where your outer beauty is reflected. It is vital that all three parts – spirit, soul and body – that make up your life as a human being, are given equal consideration. All three components of your life must be in unity and networking together, in order for you to live the abundant life God designed for you to live.

> *You can't keep doing what is wrong and hope to get a right outcome.*

Jesus clearly stated in John 10:10 that one of His purposes for coming to earth in human form was to give you a life that you could enjoy and have in abundance, to the full, till it overflows. Without receiving forgiveness and healing and allowing God to bring you to wholeness, you cannot experience the peace that Jesus came to give you.

> *'Peace I leave with you; My own peace I now give and bequeath to you. Not as the world gives, do I give to you. Do not let your hearts*

be troubled, neither let them be afraid.' [Stop allowing yourselves
to be agitated and disturbed; and do not permit yourselves
to be fearful and intimidated and cowardly and unsettled.]
(JOHN 14:27)

Without true healing in your soul, your body will, sooner or later, convey the message to the outside world of what is really taking place on the inside. No matter how great your dreams and aspirations are, if your body is in a state of disrepair and abuse, it will not be able to sustain you, to optimize your talents, in your spirit, soul or intellect.

At the time in my life when my body and mind were giving me warning signals that all was not well on the inside and that there was much repair and restoration needed, I had the privilege of someone guiding me through the challenges that we face in this life. I soon realized that there were many areas of my life that needed forgiveness, healing, deliverance and cleansing. My list of what I needed to acknowledge, repent of, turn away from, and who to forgive was pages long and I had to start with myself! The starting point had to be the renouncing of all ungodly activities in which I had dabbled as a child, within the context of my family practices and beliefs. These practices included astrology (believing some mysterious controlling and persuasive force had control over my life, instead of having faith in God). I had to turn away from involvement with the occult, which included levitation, psychic readings, astrology and playing 'glassy-glassy'. These dangerous practices had been entrenched in my family for generations. One only knows the evil power inherent in these practices, once one has experienced the strongholds of fear, torment, delusion and self-destruction and only when one has been set free from their powerful control and deception. God warns us about these destructive behaviours in the Bible.

> *It is the pent-up emotions of anger, bitterness, hurt and unforgiveness that leave one fractured, fragmented and living a distorted life.*

202

'And when the people [instead of putting their trust in God] shall
say to you, consult for direction, mediums and wizards who chirp
and mutter; should not a people seek and consult their God?
Should they consult the dead on behalf of the living? [Direct such
people] to the teaching and to the testimony! If their teachings
are not in accord with this word, it is surely because there is no
dawn and no morning for them. And they [who consult mediums
and wizards] shall pass through the land sorely distressed and
hungry and when they are hungry, they will fret, and will curse by
their king and their God; and whether they look upward or look to
the earth, they will behold only distress, and into thick darkness
and widespread, obscure night they shall be driven away.'
(ISAIAH 8:19–22)

By participating in such works of darkness, you open wide the doors for easy access by ungodly influences opposed to righteous living, and you give them the legal right to have free rein in your life. I knew many days and nights of tormented thoughts, of feeling driven to destructive acts, of experiencing the paralysis that fear brings and being deluded that I could

Dabbling with darkness leads to living a distorted life.

never be free from these strangleholds. It was as if I was passing through life sorely distressed, fearful, hungry and fretful, experiencing deep darkness. Experiencing such things, coupled with having a very insecure childhood and creating a storehouse of bad memories led to a poisonous cocktail being brewed in my soul. Unless these hidden strongholds are confronted and addressed, wholeness can never become a reality. It is the pent-up emotions of anger, bitterness, hurt and unforgiveness that leave one fractured, dysfunctional and fragmented. Dabbling with darkness leads to living a distorted life.

If you have been involved in practices that have left you in fear or torment, or have given you false hope, you need to go to God and acknowledge and turn away from these things. Renounce your entanglement with works of darkness that are totally contrary to living in the light of Jesus. Then, having turned away from them, make absolutely sure that you give no place to them in your life, now or ever again in your future. If you have consulted the stars to give you guidance, as to how you should live, think or act, close that door and refuse it entrance into your life. If you have consulted a medium or tarot card reader, repent and refuse to ever return. Furthermore, verbally cut off from your life, with determination, in the Name of Jesus, every ungodly word that has ever been spoken over your life by these people, even if the word seemed valid or correct at the time. Give no place to these practices in your life if you want to live in freedom! Through Jesus Christ you can be delivered and set free from torment and every type of bondage caused by your delving into areas that do not have their origins in the Truth of God. Life is strewn with wrecked lives whose decisions were based on what the 'cards' said, only to end up shipwrecked and stranded.

> 'But if we really are living and walking in the Light, as He Himself
> is in the Light, we have [true, unbroken] fellowship with one
> another, and the blood of Jesus Christ, His Son, cleanses us
> from all sin and guilt [keeps us cleansed from sin in all its forms
> and manifestations]. If we say we have no sin [refusing to admit
> that we are sinners], we delude and lead ourselves astray and
> the Truth [which the Gospel presents] is not in us [does not
> dwell in our hearts]. If we [freely] admit that we have sinned and
> confess our sins, He is faithful and just [true to His own nature
> and promises] and will forgive our sins [dismiss our lawlessness]
> and continuously cleanse us from all unrighteousness [everything
> not in conformity to His will in purpose, thought and action].
> If we say [claim] we have not sinned, we contradict His Word
> and make Him out to be false and a liar, and His Word is not in
> us [the divine message of the Gospel is not in our hearts].'
> (1 JOHN 1:7–10)

My life was shipwrecked as I placed my hope in a psychic and the stars as I believed they could give me direction. The result was a life of misdirected hope and fear. Fear used to be my constant negative companion. Living through a fearful childhood involving violence and aggression, ever moving from city to city, and from school to school, I had to secure full-time work at the age of 14 to contribute to a one-income household that was very debt-ridden. Early in my life I began to recognize a pattern of insecurity in myself, of attracting destructive relationships and having a terrifying fear of the future. I felt trapped and unable to escape my feelings and emotions. I became overwhelmed by the weight of unrelenting fear that pressed down on me. As the dark tunnel of no sense of self-worth or self-esteem and self-value continued its downward spiral, I found myself a constant volunteer in manipulative and controlling relationships. In young adulthood I was somewhere between merely existing and seriously contemplating death. I desperately tried to find solutions to the boiling cauldron inside that threatened to erupt and end my life at any moment. I looked to everyone and anything else for relief.

At the crisis hour of my life, one woman by the name of Jenny Ward had the courage to intercept my self-destructive road. She led me to a powerful introduction to Jesus who had me in His hands. My spirit-life and indeed my whole life was about to change forever:

Change starts with desire.

> 'For God did not give us a spirit of timidity, (of cowardice, of craven and cringing and fawning fear), but He has given us a spirit of power and of love and of calm and well-balanced mind and discipline and self-control.'
> (2 TIMOTHY 1:7)

This did not mean the end of troubles and challenges. It did mean, however, that I now had an Anchor to secure me in whatever future storms might lie ahead. To truly heal from the inside is not an overnight process but a process that can have you living life as God intended for you to live, if you will allow patience to have its perfect work. You need to trust the changes that God brings into your life. God will often allow frustration to be the driver to propel you towards change. Change is the price of survival.

> 'But let endurance and steadfastness and patience have full play and do a thorough work, so that you may be people perfectly and fully developed [with no defects], lacking in nothing.'
> (JAMES 1:4)

It is never safe to look into the future with the eyes of fear.

EDWARD HENRY HARRIMAN

My mother was always a pillar of strength in my life. She taught me the importance of pressing on and never giving up, despite the uncertainty, anxiety and disappointments we often faced in our lives. Having to leave school in Standard 6 (grade 8) to brave the big wide working world, I became skilful in projecting that all was well. A belying confidence exuded from me. I was well rehearsed at hiding what was lurking dangerously within. This mask was good cover for the insecurities and fears that were well entrenched and only just beneath the surface. By the time I was 21, the mangled mess of past suppression, pent-up insecurities, fear, anger and tension was ready to explode! I have discovered from my own experiences and personally working with many people, that we express the hidden debris in our lives in one of two ways. One is by way of an explosion, an eruption, an irrational outburst. It is those feelings expressed outwardly, projecting what you feel so deeply inwardly. This can be evidenced in screaming vocal and physical rages, uncontrolled emotional outbursts, and doing physical harm to another or yourself. The other is by way of implosion. All that is suppressed on the inside bursts, thereby notifying your physical body that the inner person needs attention. This implosion express itself in depression – which is anger without expression – and makes itself known through symptoms such as eating disorders, night sweats, irrational fears, and emotional and mental breakdowns, to name just a few. Your unresolved life issues can make you become either painfully silent or extremely violent.

The silent implosion I experienced, manifested in indescribably painful migraines, blurred vision and sleeplessness, followed by months of desperate fatigue, sunken eyes from lack of sleep and intense, uncontrollable fear, insecurity and anxiety. My weight loss caused me to appear anorexic, nausea was the order of the day, major hair loss was evidenced in my bed and in the shower, and very loose-fitting clothing indicated that I was in dire need of help. Constant fear, panic attacks and depression had me in their claws. From doctor to specialist, internal to external and psychological examinations over a protracted period revealed alarming results. They could find nothing wrong with me physically! This caused me even more distress. For when you have a physical problem you can treat it medically and surgically, but when all the bodily symptoms are there but they have no root in the physical – both they and I knew the problem lay much, much deeper.

God will never bring upon us what Jesus redeemed us from.

After months of being distraught, feeling hopeless and helpless to the point of giving up, (and I considered doing so), I ventured into a church, alone and afraid. There was no thunderbolt or streaks of lightning, but I was aware of a Presence that I had not encountered before. I wept deep convulsing sobs as months of turmoil could simply not be contained any longer. Through the blur of my tears I noticed a woman in the choir who looked to me like an Angel from Heaven. At the end of the meeting I headed towards the exit with a desperate fear that I would go out the same fearful and hopeless way I came in. But God intervened! That same beautiful woman I had seen in the choir was there to meet me and in her radiant and peaceful beauty, she placed her name and telephone number in my hand. It was then that I was convinced that she was an Angel from Heaven. How could any human being have known my state of mind? Human she was indeed, but powerful in the Hand of God! And God's desire was that I become free from the burden of fear.

*'I have told you these things, so that in Me you may have
perfect peace and confidence. In the world you have
tribulation and trials and distress and frustration; but
be of good cheer; take courage; be confident, certain,
undaunted! For I have overcome the world. I have deprived
it of power to harm you and have conquered it for you.'*
(JOHN 16:33)

It is a well-documented fact that you cannot successfully live in the present, or confidently stride into the future, until you let go of the past. The PAST keeps you:

Pending
Anxious,
in **S**uspension,
and in **T**ension!

'We can draw lessons from the past but we cannot live in it,' says Lyndon B. Johnson. Living in the past, rehearsing painful memories and allowing recurring negative thoughts and fears to cloud your mind, will keep you trapped. You are the sum total of all your thoughts, choices, words, actions and reactions. What fruit are these issues bearing in your life? What you sow is what you will reap in every area of your life. This is an immutable principle. If you are tired of going around the same mountain day after day, month in and month out, year after year, the good news is this; it is totally within your power to choose, to decide that it is time for you to cooperate with God and to work on the one and only person you can change – and that is you!

It is tempting to try to change others, instead of working on yourself. Your disappointment and frustration stem from hopes and desires that are not met.

*'Unrelenting disappointment leaves you heartsick, but
a sudden good break can turn your life around.'*
(PROVERBS 13:12)

False expectations bring disillusionment that works its way into doubt. Your misplaced expectations can't be put on someone or something that you have no control over. Even God will meet your needs or resolve your problems in a specific way, which may be different to the way you anticipated that He would.

> *Living by faith is a mystifying adventure. One that has you constantly expectant and having to make peace with the truth that you may feel you can control many things in your life, but for certain, the one person you cannot control is God. At times God really doesn't seem to make any sense.*
>
> AUTHOR UNKNOWN

The reason you often try to change others is because you have endured hurts and have had bad memories of past experiences that have taken root in your life. Your past is imprinted in your life one way or another. Since you are made up of spirit, soul and body, it is helpful to remember that all three parts of your being were alive from the day you were conceived and therefore every experience from birth to your present day has made an impact or left its mark in some way in your life.

As children, any negative action impacts our emotions and leaves us scarred, since we at a young age have not developed the skill or intellect to understand or resolve a problem rationally. For many of us, those scars are deep and the memories grave, but today is the day for alignment and healing to be released into your one very important and valuable life.

> *I believe God is managing affairs and that He doesn't need any advice from me. With God in charge, I believe everything will work out for the best in the end. So what is there to worry about?*
>
> HENRY FORD

> *Living in fear keeps you living life with the brakes on.*

Fear left unchecked and unrebuked will disrupt your destiny. Living and being controlled by a spirit of fear causes you to lose your peace. Your joy dissipates and you are stripped of your strength. Fear is powerful, seductive, manipulative and controlling. Fear is a poison that insidiously permeates your mind, your will, your heart, your emotions, and finally your health.

You can conquer almost any fear if you will only make up your mind to do so. For remember, fear doesn't exist anywhere except in the mind.

DALE CARNEGIE

How often have you found fear interfering with and interrupting your future? A sound mind is safe thinking. It denotes good judgement, disciplined thought patterns and the ability to understand and make the right decisions. It includes the qualities of self-control and self-discipline. My life consisted of endless opportunities to live in fear.

From time to time I still have to slay the giant by exercising sound thinking and by harnessing disciplined thought patterns. In times of anxiety and fear, God's hand of deliverance and protection is ever present. God covers and nurtures, nourishes and protects, even when the flurry of circumstances puts us in a spin or the seasons are so barren we wonder if we will ever feel His warmth again. Despite the times of confusing trials and the string of unanswered questions, God is always working for us, on our behalf, and always for our good.

*'He that dwells in the secret place of the most High
shall remain stable and fixed under the shadow of the
Almighty [whose power no foe can withstand].
I will say of the LORD, He is my refuge and my fortress:
my God; in Him I lean, and rely, and in Him I will
confidently trust. For then He will deliver you from the
snare of the fowler, and from the deadly pestilence.
He will cover you with His feathers, and under His*

wings you shall trust and find refuge; His truth and
His faithfulness are a shield and buckler.
You shall not be afraid of the terror of the night; nor for the arrow
[the evil plots and slanders of the wicked] that flies by day;
Nor for the pestilence that stalks in darkness; nor of the destruction
and sudden death that surprise and lay waste noonday.
A thousand shall fall at your side, and ten thousand at
your right hand; but it shall not come near you.
Only a spectator shall you be [you yourself
inaccessible in the secret place of the Most High]
as you witness the reward of the wicked.
Because you have made the LORD your refuge, even the most
High your dwelling place,
There shall no evil befall you, nor any plague
or calamity come near your tent.
For he shall give His angels especial charge over
you to accompany and defend and preserve you
in all yours ways [of obedience and service].
They shall bear you up in their hands, lest
you dash your foot against a stone.
You shall tread upon the lion and adder: the young lion and
the serpent you shall trample underfoot.
Because he has set his love upon Me, therefore will I
deliver him: I will set him on high, because he knows
and understands My Name [has a personal knowledge
of My mercy, love and kindness – trusts and relies on
Me, knowing I will never forsake him, no never].
He shall call upon Me, and I will answer him: I will be with
him in trouble; I will deliver him, and honour him.
With long life will I satisfy him, and show him my salvation.'
(PSALM 91)

My Reflections on Being Redeemed to Freedom

✧ What areas of your life are ensnared by fear? Be sure to confront your fears today and replace them with faith in God.

....

....

....

....

....

....

....

....

....

....

....

....

....

....

....

....

....

....

....

....

....

....

The Power of Forgiveness ❧

I lived through a fearful childhood marked by violence and aggression. The call to total forgiveness is hard, but true freedom and your soul's liberation are priceless. We somehow feel it is our right to hold onto those things that have hurt, harmed or humiliated us. It becomes our strategy for survival. After all, shouldn't the person feel your anger towards them, experience your retribution or know your pain? This is at the heart of unforgiveness; denying yourself freedom whilst you desperately try to make someone else pay for the pain they have caused you. The truth is that you are hurt far deeper by harbouring unforgiveness and resentment towards a person than the perceived cost of forgiving them. As with everything else in life, forgiveness is a choice. Unforgiveness imprisons you and you become captive to your own bitterness. This need for revenge can present itself in twisted emotions, mental instability and in various physical ailments. You cannot separate what is taking place in your spirit, your mind, your will, your emotions or your body. All are intimately linked.

No one can go back and make a brand new start, but you can start today and make a brand new ending.

The integration between your mind and your body creates a chain reaction. Facing up to and resolving what is taking place on the inside of you is therapeutic, provided you receive God's forgiveness, forgive yourself and move on in faith and confidence, becoming richer for the experience. By blaming others you make yourself their prisoner and until the day you are prepared to forgive, you make your life an inextricable part of theirs. It is true that issues left unresolved with one's immediate family circle will create a platform for problems in future relationships. What has happened has happened. No amount of weeping, regretting or ruminating is going to change that. Life will be hard for you if you allow yourself to become snarled up in something that cannot be changed, only forgiven. You cannot hope to hurt another through your unforgiveness and expect not to be hurt in return. The harm you do to yourself by believing that someone, or a situation, has control over you and that you cannot help the way you feel, brings inevitable despair and defeat. Believing this lie means that you will never take responsibility for the way you personally feel, because you will always be placing the blame for the way you feel, and the ways in which you react, and your life's outcomes on someone else. You have been designed by God, made in the likeness of God and He has given you one very powerful capability; the freedom to choose. Yes, you have to make the choice to forgive! It is not a feeling, but a choice that needs to be made. Sometime later the feeling may follow. Whether you feel different or not is irrelevant. What is most important is that your choice to forgive frees you from being the victim of someone else's behaviour.

> 'This day I call heaven and earth as witnesses against you that
> I have set before you life and death, blessings and curses.
> Now choose life, so that you and your children may live.'
> (DEUTERONOMY 30:19,20)

The verse quoted above clearly shows that we alone decide whether we live our lives under a blessing or under a curse. Living, by choice, with unforgiveness towards someone is choosing to live under a curse. An attractive, radiant woman stood up in one of my seminars to share the story of the release she experienced in making a quality choice to forgive. This is her personal story, used with permission. This beautiful woman had been violated in a way that left her hurt, angry and bitter towards the one who had inflicted so much pain on her. This was to such

Forgiveness is giving up your right to hurt the one who hurt you.

an extent that her life became infused and consumed with exacting vengeance. Until one day at a conference, the speaker shared of the power of release to be found in forgiving those who have knowingly, or unknowingly, hurt you.

In many instances you may not be able personally to face the one who has caused the hurt. This can be for reasons of the death of the person who caused you pain, or that you fear intimidation or retribution, or that geographic distance may separate you from the offender. In any event, the speaker offered a practical approach to dealing with people that needed to be forgiven. It was suggested she write a letter with the intention of never giving it to the person concerned. In this letter she was to express every feeling, every emotion, every thought and pain, and vent her anger, even her desire to exact vengeance. This process is painful, but it is one sure and honest way of confronting the danger that lies deep and smouldering in your soul. It is looking truth straight in the face. That which is kept in the dark becomes the enemy's territory. God can heal that which is revealed and brought into the light. God always works in truth. This letter took her two weeks to write amidst difficult emotions, anger, pain and hurt. Over this period as she put pen to paper, she began to feel the knots being untied, until she finally reached the place where she had exhausted every ounce of pent-up emotion. She folded the letter and placed it in an envelope in her wardrobe.

Don't delay; forgive today!

She awoke one night to question why she was keeping the letter. Through her ability to make a choice to let the last remnant of her anger and bitterness go forever, she removed the letter from its place and with absolute determination, tore the letter into shreds, feeling more and more released with every rip. As she shared her story it was evident that she no longer experienced the pain or the haunting memories. Anger is almost always the outworking of being hurt or rejected. She concluded her story by sharing with us that if she thinks back now, it is as if the incident never happened! This is the beauty of the release found in making the choice to forgive. Forgiving and letting go is really about you receiving your healing and your freedom. She had no control over the man who abused her, but she does have full control over how she chooses to live her life in freedom.

> 'When we hate our enemies, we are giving them power over us:
> power over our sleep, our appetites, our blood pressure, our
> health and our happiness. Our enemies would dance with joy
> if only they knew how they were worrying us, lacerating us and
> getting even with us! Our hate is not hurting them at all, but our
> hate is turning our own days and nights into a hellish turmoil.'
>
> DALE CARNEGIE

Our words and our choices are more powerful than we can imagine. The Book of Genesis clearly shows that **God** said, *'let there be'*, and there was. His Words have creative power. His written Word in the form of the Bible has the inherent power to change billions of lives and has being doing so for thousands of years. Since we are made in His Image it is no different for us. Your spoken and written words have the ability to create that which you say. What you think, see and say, will be what you get.

Your thoughts become your words and your words create what you will live through. This is why words can wound when they are spoken in anger and this creates an even greater resistance to forgiveness or relationship. However, there is not a circumstance in your life right now that cannot be positively influenced by the Word of God – the Bible, provided you choose to be obedient to His instruction. God is very clear in His instruction that we should forgive one another. If God is telling you to forgive someone, you will not be able to walk in the fullness of the blessings God has for you, until you set out to do what He has told you to do. Amongst the great exhortations of Jesus, He stresses that you forgive.

> 'Forgive their reckless and wilful sins, leaving them,
> letting them go, and giving up resentment, and
> your Heavenly Father will also forgive you.'
>
> (MATTHEW 6:14)

That's what you need to do with those who have sinned against you. Forgive everyone who has caused you hurt, humiliation or harm in any way, form or fashion. When I contemplate the price Jesus paid on the Cross at Calvary, to set me free of every offence in my life, I cannot but make a quality decision to release those who have offended me.

Hating people is like burning down your own home to get rid of a rat.

HARRY EMERSON FOSDICK

'I acknowledged my sin to You, and my iniquity I did not hide. I said, I will confess my transgressions to the Lord [continually unfold the past till all is told] then You [instantly] forgave me the guilt and iniquity of my sin.'

(PSALM 32:5)

'Be gentle and forbearing with one another and, if one has a difference [a grievance or complaint] against another, readily pardoning each other; even as the Lord has [freely] forgiven you, so must you also [forgive].'

(COLOSSIANS 3:13)

Forgiveness is giving up your right to hurt the one who hurt you. A larger portion of your life is impacted by how you react to what has been done to you than the act itself. Unforgiveness is not worth the bother, the frustration, the pain or the despair. Forgive. Let go of those things that cannot be changed. Move on. Shake the dust off your feet and choose to walk the Kingdom path of righteousness, peace and joy. Be liberated as you experience release by receiving His forgiveness within and extending forgiveness without to those who need it or who you perceive have done you harm. People need your forgiveness, just as you need God's forgiveness. You have heard it said that you

Freedom is accepting yourself because of forgiveness, which enables you to enjoy your life!

HELEN KELLER

cannot unscramble an egg. This is so, but I believe you can make an omelette out of it if you choose to! Forgiveness is for your benefit. It is about your healing and freedom. Forgiving a person does not always equate to reconciliation with that person. Extending forgiveness does not guarantee that the behaviour of the other person is ever going to change.

Neither does it mean that because you have forgiven them they will ever take ownership of their destructive behaviour. You must find a way to forgive – and live with the decision you make despite the reactions of others. Forgiving and moving on means that you never again need to be someone else's victim and that your life does not become defined by the offender. What glorious liberty! Forgiveness truly is a privilege. Forgiving someone else is one of the greatest gifts you can give yourself.

My Reflections on Forgiveness

✧ Who are the people in your life that you need to forgive?

✧ What are the issues that you need to let go?

✧ What about those secret sins or those incidents that have made you feel ashamed and guilty? A million-dollar car with all its luxury technology cannot move a centimetre, if it, for instance, has a fault in the starter motor. It is no different in your life. One secret sin can prevent the 'car of your life' from moving forward. Unforgiveness is a major hindrance. Perhaps you need to forgive yourself today.

A prayer to forgive:

Lord, today I determine to clear the clutter from my life and to take the time to forgive so I no longer remember and rehearse the hurts that have been done to me. Thank You Lord, that as I forgive, I can receive Your forgiveness and live freely justified: just as if I'd never sinned! Thank You that there is nothing that has been done to me, or that I have done, that is beyond your realm of forgiveness. Today I choose to align my life with the power of Your forgiveness and forgive those who have offended me in any and every way. Thank You Jesus for Your provision of forgiveness in my life, so that I can freely extend it to others.

Relating to God

'YOU HAVE NOT CHOSEN ME, BUT I HAVE CHOSEN YOU AND I HAVE APPOINTED YOU, [I HAVE PLANTED YOU], THAT YOU MIGHT GO AND BEAR FRUIT AND KEEP ON BEARING, AND THAT YOUR FRUIT MAY BE LASTING [THAT IT MAY REMAIN, ABIDE], SO THAT WHATEVER YOU ASK THE FATHER IN MY NAME [AS PRESENTING ALL THAT I AM], HE MAY GIVE IT TO YOU.'
(JOHN 15:16)

You have been magnificently created to be in a fulfilling relationship with God, despite some messy circumstances on earth. You are a three-in-one human being (spirit, soul and body), purposefully created by God. Your spirit is that part that God accesses to awaken in you the new birth miracle – a new way of life in and through Jesus Christ. It is the perfect exchange.

His redemption is designed to give you freedom and joy!

It is not trying to live a life of being pleasing to God, doing good works and living a life of charity only. It is a life that is abundant and filled with God's grace and the righteousness of Jesus Christ. You give back your old life to Him in exchange for His new life in you. What a trade!

You can be cleansed, made whole and have right standing with Him, right now in this moment in your life. Oh! I imagine you are thinking that I have absolutely no idea what you have done in your life or the people you have hurt, or the secret thoughts or issues you may have. Well the good news is this: there is nothing you could ever have done that cannot be cleansed by Jesus' shed Blood and His love for you. That is why He came; so you would be cleansed and made as white as snow on the inside and never need to carry around that guilt and shame again, if you will just accept His invitation and believe that He has done so:

> 'As far as the east is from the west, so far does God in
> His grace and mercy remove your sins from you.'
>
> (PSALM 103:12)

Everything you think, say, and do, forms the building blocks in constructing the kind of life upon which you will build the rest of your life. However, there is not one thought, word or action that cannot be covered by the Blood of Jesus. It is not too late! His redemption is designed to give you freedom and joy. All God requires is that you recognize and take ownership of what needs to change in your life. Make a quality decision to turn your back on an empty and unfulfilling lifestyle that can keep you from the magnificent life He offers. The Christ Life is not about striving to do what you are unable to do, but rather calling for His help and assistance when you do revert to old behaviour and destructive life patterns. When you are quick to open your heart to His prompting of your wrongdoing, He is quick to share His mercy and pardon – and He is quick to forget.

> *Undress your soul at night, by shedding as you do your garments, the daily sins whether of omission or commission, and you will wake a free man with a new life.*
>
> SIR WILLIAM OSLER

'But I, yes I, am the One Who takes care of your sins – that's what I do. I don't keep a list of your sins'.

(ISAIAH 43:25)

This is good news indeed. This is not the kind of news that you will hear on 24/7 news channels, but it is news that can forever change your life for the better.

Your spirit is the heart of your communication with God. Because you are spirit, soul and body, all three parts are actively involved in your relationship with God. Your spirit is your inner being, your source of intuition and the avenue to your conscience. If your spirit is not awakened and made alive to God, and to the potential of a spiritual life in Christ, you can remain 'dead' all life long. Unless you are fully functional in all three arenas, you run the risk of merely existing; there will always be an empty space, a void, the sense of something missing in your life. God's plan for your life is far greater than just existence. Jesus came that you might have life – not just a mediocre one, but an abundant life (John 10:10). A life with Jesus is filled with abundance and multiplication, joy unspeakable and full of glory. If you could see the life that God has planned for you, you would be prepared to give up the life you have fought for and wrestled to create for yourself.

God is a warmly personal God. He doesn't work with us by remote control from somewhere in outer space. He is deeply involved, interested and committed to you living and fulfilling His predetermined plan for your life. God does not require perfect people to come to Him. He invites the flawed; the torn and battle-scarred, the weary and disillusioned; all who will come, to receive His gift of salvation. Salvation is a gift of deliverance, rescue and recovery towards wholeness, peace, joy, overcoming and a future filled with hope.

Your worth to God was established when He formed you. God wants you to experience the joy of abiding relationship that comes from being in His Presence. His Presence equips you to impart His love, joy and peace into all the relationships in which you are involved in life. He desires that you take all that you are and all that you can become in Him, into all your relationships at every level. This is true influence. This is being a witness for Christ. Being a witness is just that. The Bible does not say a word about 'doing' a witness for Jesus. 'Being' is knowing Him, resting in Him, being at peace, and influencing others. Being is the very nature or essence of Christ in you, your hope of Glory. Being in His Presence allows you to know Him progressively more intimately. We all need individually to forge our own personal relationship with God, but it is not for us to impose this relationship on anyone else. This relationship cannot be transferred or given away; it is something that each person needs to cultivate personally. Every person needs their own visitation from God to create their own testimony. God is a God of the individual and no one else can relate to God the way you relate to

> *What's on Your agenda today, Lord? May J be part of it?*
>
> Dr Robert Schuller

Him. He values your uniqueness. Fulfilling relationships are built by spending quality, meaningful time with one another and honouring each other enough to make time for each other.

> *'Cultivate your own relationship with God, but don't impose it*
> *on others. You're fortunate if your behaviour and your beliefs*
> *are coherent. But if you're not sure, if you notice that you are*
> *acting in ways inconsistent with what you believe – some days*
> *trying to impose your opinions on others, other days just trying*
> *to please them – then you know you're out of line. If the way you*
> *live isn't consistent with what you believe, then it's wrong.'*
> (ROMANS 14:22–23)

It may be that you consider your life ordinary and unimpressive, lacking star-studded qualities and without much to offer; but God sees it otherwise. He knows what He has created and He has personally said that it is good. God doesn't need a 10-page, highly degreed and academic résumé, or the diplomas and certificates that grace the walls of many academics. All He requires is you – just as you are – just as He created you. Leave the craftsmanship to Him. Out of the unshapely mass of the clay of your life, He can create a masterpiece; a masterpiece that has more value than the entire world's wealth. Entrust your piece of clay into the Master Potter's Hands today and see if you don't marvel at the outcome! You really do matter to God. Becoming a Christian does not mean instant perfection, but it does mean instant acceptance. Salvation is God's expressed love for you and it is His way of journeying with you in this life, taking you to a destination of His choosing, so you don't derail yourself in the challenges that life often presents to you.

God desires for you to be rooted, grounded and established in Him. Your true fulfilment in this life is derived from being in that 24-hour, uninterrupted, include-God-in-everything companionship. If you would allow God to deeply intercept your life, you would begin to know His heartbeat in most situations that confront you. He desires to lead you by His Holy Spirit every second of your life. He longs for you to be in step

223

with His plan and purpose for you, and for you to fulfil your God-given assignment each day. His desire is for you always to be at the right place at the right time. He wants to open doors for you and give you the courage to walk through those doors, despite how unqualified or unprepared you may feel. If God felt you were unprepared, He would not allow the door to open. God's doesn't want you to be anxious, but truly to know and believe that your life is in His care.

> *'Giving thanks to the Father, Who has qualified and made us fit*
> *to share the portion which is the inheritance of the saints (God's*
> *holy people) in the Light. [The Father] has delivered and drawn*
> *us to Himself out of the control and the dominion of darkness*
> *and has transferred us into the kingdom of the Son of His love.'*
>
> (COLOSSIANS 1:11–13)

Do not fret or have any anxiety about anything, but in every circumstance and in everything, by prayer and petition [definite requests], with thanksgiving, continue to make your wants known to God.

(PHILIPPIANS 4:6)

A life worth living is a life that can **stand tall** in a falling world, a life not restricted by the cares and concerns of this world, and without condemnation; free from the entanglements that would stunt your growth. A life worth living is a life that is far more concerned about what God thinks than what your neighbours might think. A life worth living is about the joy of knowing that your life has God's seal of approval on it and the sell-by date will never expire. A life worth living is a life that is set by God's agenda and not your own. I am always mindful of the great Dr Robert Schuller, who daily rises and asks God, 'What's on your agenda today Lord? May I be part of it?' Do it well even if it is only of little significance to you. It is when we are faithful in the small things that He can trust us with more of His Agenda. Heed His instruction for today. Leave tomorrow in His hands.

My Reflections on Relating to God

✧ Living life with God is one of the most satisfying relationships you will ever have on earth. Your life will take on dimensions you never dreamed possible. For then you see your life not only according to your limited earthly vision, but also with His eternal panoramic vision. What are you waiting for?

Talking with God 🕊

PRAYER CHANGES THINGS. PRAYER CHANGES THE ONE PRAYING. PRAYER CHANGES THE ONE BEING PRAYED FOR.

> *Talking to God, known as prayer, is as effortless as breathing in and out.*

Standing tall in a falling world that is being torn apart by rebellion, power-hungry, unscrupulous dictators, a worldwide economy shaking from excessive consumerism, sky-high oil prices and the looming energy shortage, coupled with religious factions feuds and fundamentalism, requires that you dig deep foundations that will enable you to stand tall in the midst of the most extreme disruptions that may affect you. Foundational to this is your relationship with God; acknowledging that He is deeply personal and intricately concerned about all the matters of your life. You need to include Him in your life 24/7 and ask Him about the decisions and changes that will influence your life; past, present and future. Talking to God, also known as prayer, is as effortless as breathing in and out. I

> *Relationship is a way of being. Religion is a form of doing.*

know that the idea of talking in conversational day-to-day language with a God who, in one breath, can create a new realm of galaxies, is a little daunting to say the least, but that is how accepting He is of you and me. Prayer requires respect, thoughtful interaction, and listening. It doesn't require the Queen's English or a special voice to pray in. God enjoys you just as you are, after all, that is the way

He made you. It is vital to take time to shut out the noise of the world, and spend time focusing on God. The only way you can build sustainable relationships on this earth is to spend time with the people you want to know more intimately. Well, it is exactly the same in developing a relationship with God. He is available to meet with you in your car, in the shower, in the kitchen or while you are lying on your bed. Having a relationship with Almighty God is not the same as being religious with God. Relationship is a way of being. Religion is a form of doing. It is interesting to note that Jesus' disciples never asked Him to teach them to preach, but rather to teach them how to pray. Prayer is a lifestyle. It is the art of carrying a spirit of prayer (talking with God) into all aspects of life. Prayer is a heart attitude that is sometimes not even expressed in words. Union with God comes from unbroken, constant communion with Him. Deep communion with God will require times of solitude when you shut out the clutter and clamour of the world and you become still, knowing full well that He is God. Talking with God is your lifeline. Prayer always gets through to God.

Prayers made in faith are sure deposits made into your Heavenly bank account. God's account is always open and prayer is His way of giving you a blank cheque and is an invitation to you to 'draw from Him what we need'. It is your faith that determines the amount. The Bible, which is the Heavenly Book of Account, tells you that the amount available to you is without limit; for with God everything is possible. You need never fear having to go into overdraft, and your withdrawals will always be honoured, because they are made in the mighty Name of Jesus and you are the bearer of that Name.

Study of the Bible, His Word, is paramount for your life to stay on track.

> 'All Scripture is God-breathed and is useful for teaching, rebuking, correcting and training in righteousness, so that the man of God may be thoroughly equipped for every good work.'
> (2 TIMOTHY 3:16–17)

Making a conscious effort to meditate on God and His Word will allay many of your fears and prevent your stresses during the day. Find the promises that relate to your circumstances and stand tall, making a decision not to get weak at the knees, to waver, or buckle, when natural circumstances and outcomes seem to contradict the Word of God. Make a point of listening to uplifting teachings, music and conversations. If you are going to stand tall in this falling world, you have to make a sound decision to remove yourself from negative and destructive activities, and topics of conversation. My husband always says that when you meet someone negative, you never walk away from them. You run away from them as fast as possible before they make you negative too! Negative people will negate and undermine what you believe and what you stand for. Don't fall on account of someone else's cynicism, critical spirit or negative approach to life. To stand tall when everything else threatens to bring you down is a courageous choice and it's worth the effort.

> '*I have told you these things, so that in Me you may have*
> *[perfect] peace and confidence. In the world you have*
> *tribulation and trials and distress and frustration; but*
> *be of good cheer [take courage; be confident, certain,*
> *undaunted]! For I have overcome the world. [I have deprived*
> *it of power to harm you and have conquered it for you.]*'
> (JOHN 16:33)

Acknowledging your need of Jesus as Lord of your life keeps you in a place of humility; knowing that without God you cannot accomplish anything of substance and eternal value. Staying close to God by continuous communication, just as you would speak to a person who is in your company, will help you through the many trials, tests, tribulations and temptations that you will face in your lifetime. Without the close, continuous communication with God, life can become overwhelming and leave you with a sense that your life is unravelling. There is no substitute for spending time in the Presence of God. Include Him in the little details of your life and He will bring you much joy, peace, direction, hope and confidence.

> '*To clasp the hands in prayer is the beginning of an*
> *uprising against the disorder of the world.*'
> KARL BATH

My Reflections on Talking to God

✧ Be ultra-aware over the next 24 hours of being in the Presence of God. Take note of the difference it makes to you and your life.

✧ God is closer to you than your own skin. If you have never talked to God before, there is no time like the present.

In Quietness and in Confidence ❧

IN QUIETNESS AND IN TRUSTING CONFIDENCE SHALL BE YOUR STRENGTH.
(ISAIAH 30:15)

Waiting for the commencement of a vision, a dream, or a desire you were so sure would come to pass, can be amongst the most challenging of experiences in life. In that place of 'Divine Suspension', the temptation to look at the realities of your life with despondency and downheartedness can be overbearing. There are many voices in the world that would tell you that if you're not in frenetic, non-stop activity, you're not accomplishing. The concept of waiting in this high-speed information age is foreign to us. We often feel guilty for allegedly 'doing nothing'. To be further afflicted, it seems that others notice our obvious levels of inactivity and try to sweep us along with their chaotic lives. Yet

He has planned for your success; your welfare and your future; not your failure.

we honour God because being still and withdrawing for a while is an act of trust, and we can enjoy the reward that follows when we get off the bullet train, stop and take in our surroundings; breathe deeply and find some quietness. In quietness we can confidently say our strength is being renewed.

Often you are so busy speeding through life that even if the opportunity to reach your dream confronted you today, you would miss it.

Standing tall in your life demands that you discipline yourself to take time out – you may even need forcibly to take yourself out of the hubbub of activities that have become such a habit, so that you can be still, listen and be in restful trust. Then, when your time comes to see the dawning of your dream or desire, you will be better equipped and able, with the right perspective, to carry out what you have been designed to do. Fierce activity clutters your spirit and soul until you cannot distinguish good from bad or sound judgement from poor. Not only can you have an overactive mind and body, but also agitation in your spirit. Instead of being at peace and at rest, there is constantly impatience and irritation swirling around on the inside of you. This is a good time to be reminded that God always purposes every circumstance for your good. His perfect plan is not to release you into a mission that you are not ready to undertake. He has planned for your success, not your failure.

It's time to take the dust off your trust!

> 'For I know the plans I have for you,' declares
> the LORD, 'plans to prosper you and not to harm
> you, plans to give you hope and a future.'
> (JEREMIAH 29:11)

There is always the danger of running ahead of God, being untrained and unprepared, the consequences of which can be dire. Take a moment to see the preparation David endured before he became king. David was chosen to be king as a young boy, yet he spent many years being a shepherd boy. He watched his brothers go to war, and still he kept shepherding. He had to fight off the lion and the bear. He waited and endured much opposition before he could enter into the fullness of what God had planned for him. The trademark of David's life as evidenced in his poetry in the Psalms, was that he waited in quietness and confidence, in praise and in worship, and with trust in God's plan, despite the major challenges that pursued him throughout his life. Moses was in the wilderness for 40 years – talk about quiet times – but those times were the preparation material for the greatest event not only in his life, but for the future of the nation of Israel! Esther went through intense preparation to fulfil the call on her life. She was raised from orphan to queen and it required that she spend many years in quietness and in confidence. The time of your deepest preparation, and sometimes your greatest frustration, is when you are seemingly idle. Resting in trust makes the greatest demand on your faith. But the joy of release when God says, 'Now go!' makes you able to complete the tasks set before you with effortless ease.

*'For thus said the Lord God, the Holy One of Israel: In returning
to Me and resting in Me you shall be saved; in quietness
and in trusting confidence shall be your strength.'*
(ISAIAH 30:15)

The alarming end to this verse says, *'but you would not'*. Every one of God's promises comes with a call to obedience. God won't give you another instruction until you have obeyed the last one. When you wait in quietness and in confidence, you are availing yourself of His inner work; a renovation and reconstruction of the inner-person who will reflect God to the world. To wait is to trust. The two are inseparably linked. It's time to take the dust off your trust. Know that it is in those times of quiet, in the hidden days, your dreams and desires were being birthed. In the quietness, your thoughts, passions, desires, purposes and plans for your life were being aligned, giving you hope, despite the challenges of your day-to-day situations. Your God-dream will drive you through the storms of life. Holding onto your hope will help you smooth over obstacles, yield to change and enable you to flex in those trying situations. You know you have been created for much more than you have settled for. Your dream will tarry, however, until you get to the place of knowing that He is in control of your life. When you take hold of His agenda and let go of your own, you get past the disappointments that come from enforcing your own will, and realize that, apart from Him, you can do nothing of eternal value anyway, and only then will your dreams become your reality.

God's eternal words will never fail in the short term or in the longer term.

God's perfectly timed seasons come as a result of His deep personal pruning in your life. The season for release comes about when you have endured – yes, sometimes dangerously close to the twelfth hour, but you have endured nonetheless. Not one of God's words has ever failed. He simply says it and that settles it. You can take it as His promise because God cannot lie. His integrity is beyond reproach. You can receive it as a promise, because He said it. God can be totally and completely trusted in every area of your life. The fulfilment of your dream will be powered by your submission to God's processes and to His timing and agenda.

> 'Roll your works upon the Lord [commit and trust them wholly
> to Him; He will cause your thoughts to become agreeable
> to His will], and so shall your plans be established and
> succeed. The Lord has made everything to accommodate
> itself and contribute to its own end and His own purpose.'
>
> (PROVERBS 16:3,4,10)

My Reflections on Quietness and Confidence

✧ Stop, pause, breathe, rest and listen. You will be amazed at what you will receive when you take a moment to get off the treadmill of life. You owe this to yourself.

Abiding Under the Shadow of the Almighty 🌿

'HE WHO DWELLS IN THE SECRET PLACE OF THE MOST HIGH SHALL REMAIN STABLE AND FIXED UNDER THE SHADOW OF THE ALMIGHTY [WHOSE POWER NO FOE CAN WITHSTAND].'
(PSALM 91:1)

The greatest enemy of your life is fear. It has been said 'there is nothing to fear except fear itself'. Fear left unchecked and unresisted will disrupt your peace of mind, your ability to choose and even your destiny. Living and being controlled by a spirit of fear causes you to lose your peace. Your joy dissipates and you are stripped of your strength. Fear is seductive, manipulative and controlling. Fear is a poison that insidiously permeates your mind and heart, and it can work its way into your physical being, often identified as symptoms of stress. How often have you found fear interfering with your present and your future? For more than half my life I have taken ownership of the following weapon found in the armoury of Scripture. I still use it when I am confronted by any suggestion to be fearful of someone or some circumstance:

Standing tall in a falling world requires sound thinking, good judgement and discernment.

> 'For God has not given us a spirit of fear, but of
> power and of love and of a sound mind.'
> (2 TIMOTHY 1:7)

Standing tall in a falling world requires that you have sound thinking, good judgement and discernment. A sound mind means you have peace, and the ability to understand and to make the right decisions. It includes the qualities of self-control and self-discipline in your thought life. Soundness of mind is a place of safety, where your life is not constantly sabotaged by fearful and intimidating thoughts. My life consisted of endless opportunities to live in fear. From time to time I still have to slay the giant. Once you have a plan of action to confront your spirit of fear, you can live in that place of perfect peace. These three 'Rs' need to become your weapons of mass destruction, so that when you sense your enemy of fear lurking close by, you can automatically press the button and launch into attack against your menacing foe.

The first 'R' is to **RECOGNIZE** how fear gains access into your thought life. Remember we often fear the suggestion of fear, more than fearing the actual circumstance. Negative images create an experience of fear. Fear begins as a little seed that is sown into your mind. What you see is what you get. The fear can be rooted in a memory, a past experience, an apprehension about something, or a forthcoming event that makes you 'nervous'. A little anxious thought can very quickly turn into stomach-churning worry, and before long it turns into raw fear, where your peace of mind is absent, your thoughts are scrambled and your ability to make a sound decision is seriously impaired. Recognizing this enemy is the first step to overcoming it! You cannot confront what you do not recognize. See it for what it is. Start thinking, imagining, speaking and acting on what you do want and not what you don't want.

Secondly you must **RESIST** the thought – the images in your mind. Resist aloud the invasion of fear that attempts to come upon you. It is also wise to remember that if you are opening your life to images that cause you to fear – such as watching television programmes or movies, or reading material that conjures up fearful images – only you can take control of what you feed your mind. Fear and harmony cannot abide together. Fear is the opposite of faith. You have to resist and root out what is going to undermine or destroy you. You become what you focus on. Press on in faith and learn to gain the territory that will give you ever-increasing victory. Your soundness of mind is worth it!

Lastly, **REFUSE** to dwell on any thoughts, memories or images that cause you to be anxious and fearful in any way. You have the authority to decide what can and cannot come into your mind. 'You can't stop the birds from flying around your head, but you certainly can stop them from nesting there!' If you give fear access, your fears will become a self-fulfilling prophecy; you constantly reinforce what you are fearful of either by playing it over in your mind or speaking about it. Fear then keeps presenting itself in your life, again making you believe that the thing you fear will come upon you! You must choose to refuse! Your choice today to refuse those fearful thoughts can change your life from fearful to one of glorious freedom from fear!

The significant problems we face cannot be solved by the same level of thinking that created them.

ALBERT EINSTEIN

The secret to living in perfect peace is abiding under His Shadow, living in the Presence of God, and keeping your mind steadfast on Him. Renew your mind with fresh, faith-filled thinking each day. When your mind is God-filled it is very difficult for it to be fear-filled. There is a wonderful promise in Isaiah 26:3, *'You will keep him in perfect peace, because his mind is stayed on you, because he trusts in you.'*

My Reflections on Living Free From Fear

✧ What causes you to stray into fearful territory and lose your peace?

✧ What is going to be your mechanism to recognize the temptation to fear?

✧ How will you sustain freedom from fear in your own life? Practise replacing fear-filled thoughts with God's Word and His thoughts, especially focusing on what He thinks of you.

The Way of Wisdom ✒

'WISDOM SPEAKS OF EXCELLENT THINGS.'
(PROVERBS 8:6)

Wisdom is one of the keys that will open the door for you to live a great life. Gaining wisdom means that you live with increased understanding and you expand your knowledge of the ways of life; you gain insight and a shift in your perception of life and people takes place. Wisdom brings astuteness, intelligence increases, and acumen is heightened; good judgement stands on the shoulders of wisdom.

> 'For wisdom is better than rubies, and all the things one may
> desire cannot be compared with her. "I, wisdom, dwell with
> prudence, and find out knowledge and discretion. The fear
> of the LORD is to hate evil; pride and arrogance and the evil
> way and the perverse mouth I hate. Counsel is mine, and
> sound wisdom. I am understanding, I have strength."'
> (PROVERBS 8:11–14)

> 'Wisdom is the principal thing; therefore get wisdom. And
> in all your getting, get understanding. Exalt her (wisdom)
> and she will promote you; she will bring you honour when
> you embrace her. She will place on your head an ornament
> of grace; a crown of glory she will deliver to you.'
> (PROVERBS 4:7–9)

Wisdom is knowing the truth and how to apply it to every situation or circumstance you encounter in your life. When you have wisdom and you share it with others, even their circumstances will change as they apply your insight into their lives. Because wisdom is linked to the fear of the Lord – not a trembling, terrifying fear, but a respectful, and honour-filled approach to the Lord – and because you honour God as the primary Source of your life, wisdom and understanding flow from that relationship. However, wisdom and understanding will only flow from a heart that hates evil. God's wisdom and evil cannot abide in one heart.

The one you relate to the most will be the most dominant.

The doors of wisdom are never shut.

BENJAMIN FRANKLIN

'*The fear of the Lord is the beginning of wisdom, and the knowledge of the Holy One is understanding. For by me your days will be multiplied, and years of life will be added to you.*'

(PROVERBS 9:10,11)

The wisdom in walking in the fear of the Lord is based on acknowledging that He has placed certain laws within the earth that need to be obeyed. Without obeying these laws, consequences can remain for the duration of your life, if not for generations. These laws were put there for your ultimate protection and safety. To obey Him is to honour Him and to trust that He, the Creator, knows what is best for His creation. Knowing that you will harvest what you have sown should be one of the foundational principles of your life, which must surely encourage you to live with a healthy fear of the Lord. God is not mocked – what we sow is what we will reap.

The time is always right to do the right thing.

MARTIN LUTHER KING JR.

Wisdom is to know God's will and to do it!

'*Wisdom is the principal thing: therefore get wisdom. And in all your getting get understanding.*'

(PROVERBS 4:7)

Standing tall in a falling world demands wisdom be applied in every area of your life.

Living with Wisdom Creates Wealth

'Riches and honour are with me, enduring riches and righteousness. My fruit is better than gold, yes, than fine gold, and my revenue than choice silver. I traverse the way of righteousness, in the midst of the paths of justice, that I may cause those who love me to inherit wealth, that I may fill their treasuries.'
(PROVERBS 8:18–21)

'He who has a slack hand becomes poor but the hand of the diligent makes rich.'
(PROVERBS 10:4)

'The blessing of the Lord makes one rich, and He adds no sorrow with it.'
(PROVERBS 10:22)

Living with Wisdom Creates the Potential for Long Life

'For by me your days will be multiplied, and years of life will be added to you.'
(PROVERBS 9:11)

'The fear of the Lord prolongs days, but the years of the wicked will be shortened.'
(PROVERBS 10:27)

Living with Wisdom Causes You to Speak Right

'The mouth of the righteous is a well of life.'
(PROVERBS 10:11)

'Wisdom is found on the lips of him who has understanding.'
(PROVERBS 10:13)

*'Wise people store up knowledge but the mouth
of the foolish is near destruction.'*
(PROVERBS 10:14)

*'In the multitude of words sin is not lacking,
but he who restrains his lips is wise.'*
(PROVERBS 10:19)

'The tongue of the righteous is choice silver.'
(PROVERBS 10:20)

*'The lips of the righteous feed many, but
fools die for lack of wisdom.'*
(PROVERBS 10:21)

'The mouth of the righteous brings forth wisdom.'
(PROVERBS 10:31)

'The lips of the righteous know what is acceptable.'
(PROVERBS 10:32)

*Lord, may I always have a wise answer on my tongue. Help me
always to roll my works upon You, to commit and trust them
wholly to You. May my thoughts always become agreeable
to Your will and may Your blessing be upon my plans so that
they may be established and succeed. Let me always depart
from and avoid evil. I ask that my ways so please You that even
my enemies will be at peace with me. May Divinely directed
decisions be on my heart and lips, so that I never transgress in
judgement. I ask for skilful and Godly wisdom more than I ask for
gold. Release understanding to me more than silver. Help me to
guard my ways so that my life will be preserved. May I always be
wise in heart, be full of understanding – knowing that winsome
speech increases knowledge both to the speaker and to the
hearer. Let pleasant words bring healing to my body. Amen.*

My Reflections on Living My Life with Wisdom

- ❖ Exchange your lack for His wealth because of His wisdom.
- ❖ Ask for long life as you make a decision to walk in His wisdom.
- ❖ Exchange your life-shortening words for His life-giving words.

Working with The King 🌿

The reality of Christianity is Jesus Christ alive on this earth through you and me. We all have times of deep dissatisfaction with life; but that is often a signal that your circumstances are about to change. Dissatisfaction drives you deeper into your destiny. Destiny, simply put, is what 'you were designed to be'! Without dissatisfaction you would never have a signal to move on. Life becomes ho-hum and boring if you mark time doing the same old things each day.

People will know that Jesus is alive on this earth when they see Him in you!

If you were a newspaper how would your headline read? If people were reading the fine print, let them not be reading yesterday's news of grouching and complaining, of disappointment and disillusionment. Rather let them read of current change and hope emblazoned by your faith. Let them read of your life progressively overcoming and **standing tall** even when the world appears to be falling.

You have been given many inherent gifts and your destiny is designed for you alone to fulfil. Your gifts are the empowered ability to do things that only you can do with your personality and talents; you are seasoned with God's grace to release your gifts, and you have an anointing – a Divine enabling to do what only you can do! No one else can exercise and share your gifts the way you can. Whether you preach, teach, serve, administrate, share your hospitality, whether you are in business, or you fly an aircraft, or care for young children or older folk; whatever you do, there is a uniqueness in your way of carrying out your gift that no one else in the world can replicate. (See 1 Corinthians 12). Ministry is service overflowing with love and ability. Ministry

Keep God's sovereignty and your responsibility in balance.

is doing what you do every day for God and for others. Ministry is not a place, a position or a profile. Ministry is a lifestyle. Ministry is about being available and willing as an instrument in the Hands of God to accomplish His plans and purposes on the earth.

Many try different formulas, programmes, and even someone else's styles and approaches to 'do the work of the ministry'. Yet God has a more simple way – a non-pressured way – a naturally spiritual way. People will know that Jesus is alive on this earth when they see Him in you! People don't enjoy being preached at but they will listen to someone sharing. Your sharing may be wordless and soundless, yet people will know you are overflowing with love because of your actions. One missionary was known to have said, 'Share Jesus with the people you meet and use words only if you have to!' You can only share Jesus with others to the degree that He possesses you. Share the bread of your life with them that they may taste and see that the Lord is good. Your greatest asset is your testimony to the love and power of God at work in your own life. When you have fed others with the Bread of Life, they too will hunger for more of God, knowing that they too can be filled to overflowing. Forcing your beliefs down people's throats causes them to gag. Many people close their ears to this type of force-feeding because they have been nauseated by religious fervour and legalistic condemnation. Judgemental, inflexible and strong mindsets have created barriers to people experiencing God as a loving, gentle and understanding Father. Many people have had encounters with religion that close their natural and spiritual ears. A great number have had negative experiences carried out 'in the Name of God'. Through all of the different circumstances people have been exposed to, our responsibility is simply to break the Bread of Life with them, allowing each one to digest what is palatable to them. All then get fed the right amounts at the right time. People don't necessarily need to hear the word from our lips – they want to experience His touch in their lives. It is worthwhile remembering that Jesus said,

*'No one is able to come to Me unless the Father Who sent
Me attracts and draws him and gives him the desire to
come to Me, and then I will raise him up at the last day.'*
[JOHN 6:44]

It is God's responsibility to save people; it is our responsibility to share our lives. Other religions say 'do', Jesus says 'done!' Let's keep God's sovereignty and our responsibility in balance. **Standing tall** in a falling world requires that you take the decision to remember your humanity and thank God for His Sovereignty. As you go about your business today, whatever that may be, be mindful of the fact that you are His mouthpiece, His hands, His feet, and you are representing Jesus. Be obedient to what He asks you to do today. Do it with joy, do it with effortless ease for *'The Kingdom of God is righteousness, peace and joy in the Holy Spirit.'* (Romans 14:17)

> *It is God's responsibility to save people; it is our responsibility to share our lives.*

Life in Christ is a liberated life, a joyous life. He never said we wouldn't experience hardships and tribulations but in it all He is the Captain of our souls. Charter your course using Jesus as your only Compass. Following any other direction could mean the sinking of your ship and of those around you, because they too need the hope of the abundant life that Christ gives. Jesus is your Anchor, the Creator of your destiny – the Creator of who you were designed to be, and the One Who will bring you to a safe haven in all the storms of life. There is no greater fulfilment than working in tandem with the King!

My Reflections on Working with The King

✧ Don't limit God or yourself by mistakenly believing that you don't have gifts that can make a difference to this world.

✧ There is nothing that you and God cannot accomplish today.

Holy Spirit – Holy Life ✌

ALL THINGS ARE POSSIBLE TO HIM WHO BELIEVES.

A part from the purpose of God we really can't achieve anything of lasting value. This does not mean we can't do anything. Daily we can do tons of 'stuff'. Knowing that which has eternal value and applying it, however, keeps us from doing the immaterial. Knowing that you can do all things through Christ who strengthens you is one thing, but it is another thing entirely to know that unless God's seal of approval is on it, all you will produce is wood, hay and stubble. You need to be moving from your agenda to God's blueprint for your life. This reminds me of what Dr Robert Schuller of the Crystal Cathedral Church in Anaheim, California, shares in his book, *Prayer: My Soul's Adventure with God*. As he awakens each day he asks God, 'What's on your agenda today Lord? May I be part of it?' Discover what God desires for you to do on this day, at this moment. Do it. Do it even if it is only seemingly of little significance. Do it to the best of your ability. Do it with excellence. Do it even if it doesn't make sense to you. Do it even when it makes you feel afraid. When you are faithful in the small things, He can trust you with more of what is on His agenda. Know His heart for you today. Heed the instruction for today. Leave tomorrow in His hands.

Your greatest victories are won from a place of rest. This does not necessarily equate to everything around you being calm. In the midst of the circumstances there is a place deep within where the Spirit of God resides, and it is finding this place that brings you through to completion, victory and restoration. I remember reading about an art competition where the artists were called upon to depict scenery of restful and absolute peace. Many submissions were of mountain ranges, snow-tipped peaks or yachts on a calm ocean. The artist who won created a scene of a raging

> *His Presence will keep you standing tall in a falling world.*

storm blowing hard against a large tree that had become bent over and was fast losing its leaves to a fierce rainstorm. This tree housed a bird that had just built a nest for her young. In the midst of this storm she was protecting her chicks – unmoved, trusting and calm. In that place of rest she knew in time that storm too would pass. This is the place of trust; the place where God desires for you to be at rest. You can take God at His Word. Having received a promise from Him, enter it by faithfully declaring and believing His Word for you and then daily put one foot faithfully in front of the other and inherit His promise just for you. Walk in faith, run in hope. As you are positioned in rest you will sleep in perfect peace, fully assured that He can accomplish that which He promised. His Presence is the only antidote to living in a world of turmoil. In His Presence is fullness of joy. His Presence will keep you **standing tall** in a falling world.

> 'You will guard him and keep him in perfect and constant
> peace whose mind [both in its inclination and its
> character] is stayed on You because he commits himself
> to You, leans on You and hopes confidently in You.'
> (ISAIAH 26:3)

The more you are entrenched in God and the more deeply He dwells in you, the higher the level of authority you attain. The overcoming life is for the one who lives, moves and has their being in God. You and I are to be Jesus' eyes, His mouth, His hands and feet. Before Jesus was resurrected into Glory, He promised that His Father would send the Holy Spirit. When you are filled with the Holy Spirit, He releases within you the power for Kingdom employment. To be employed by God is the most satisfying work you can do. God's organization is not ever only in the church, but also in the workplace, in schools, in politics, in the arts and media, in business, and in a variety of other areas that make up life on earth as we know it. The rewards

Those who know their God will do mighty exploits – don't get spiritually satisfied.

for being employed by God are superb and the retirement benefits are out of this world! You as a believer give expression to the Christ who lives in you by the Holy Spirit. Surrender your physical, mental and emotional faculties to Jesus in order for Him to be represented through you to a world in dire need. The Apostle Paul said,

'It is no longer I who live, but Christ lives in me.'
(GALATIANS 2:20)

You can only reproduce what you are. You cannot give what you don't have. What a challenge to pursue Christ-likeness! Those who know their God will do mighty exploits – don't become spiritually satisfied.

Dissatisfaction is your call to total relinquishment, giving up trying to control your life and everyone and everything else around you. Being in control is really a figment of your imagination. When you bring it down to bare metal, control is something we don't have. Think about it, you cannot even control your hairstyle on some days! Total surrender is a choice that every believer needs to make at some point in their lives. Your life in Christ was never meant to be lived without the empowering Living Spirit of Jesus Christ abiding in you.

Relationship with the Holy Spirit is the sweetest experience on earth. He is the Gentleman of all gentlemen. He will never violate your free will. He will never cajole, connive or force you into anything. He responds to your need of Him, your welcoming invitation.

True relationship cannot be forced on anyone.

True relationship cannot be forced on anyone. The Holy Spirit works through the believer to accomplish that which brings glory to Jesus. He leads us into all truth about God, His Son and the Kingdom. He teaches us all things pertaining to life in Christ. He comforts us with the words of Jesus and brings to remembrance the very words of God. He convicts but never condemns. His desire is for us to turn away from our sinful deeds, return to Him and be cleansed by the Blood of Jesus. Sin causes one to hide from the presence of God. Sin will take you out of the presence of the Lord. Remember that you cannot confront the enemies pursuing your life when sin prevails in your life. It is like asking someone to pray for your sore foot while you have a stone in your shoe.

The Holy Spirit is our Advocate before God: He desires to see us vindicated before the Father. When I looked up the word advocate in the thesaurus, I got an even clearer picture of how committed the Holy Spirit is to championing our cause before God. An advocate is a supporter, a backer, promoter, believer, activist, campaigner, sponsor and one who is in favour of another. No one can say 'Jesus is Lord', except by revelation of the Holy Spirit. The Spirit goes before you to prepare the way for you to live. It is through the Holy Spirit that people are Born Again into a new life in Christ, and receive the Baptism of the Holy Spirit to live a holy life, a powerful life, just a whole new way of living! The power of Jesus is the Holy Spirit. Jesus said those that belong to Him would do greater works than He did, not because we are more powerful, but because the Holy Spirit is omnipotent and sovereign, and He works the works of Jesus through millions of believers. Come Holy Spirit, come! The Kingdom of God is the Kingdom of right relationships. Rejection never makes for right relationships.

Religion is a way of doing something – an act. Relationship is being part of, being one, being in unity, and being in partnership. Jesus is the soul-ution to all of our relational needs. No person can be all things to all people. Only Jesus can.

Jesus is the Soul-ution to all of our relational needs.

You don't need to go far beyond your front door to see that the people surrounding you are in desperate need of a Saviour. People's lives are ruled by fears within and without, arising from circumstances beyond their ability to handle. These people may find temporary relief from a number of sources. The only lasting, worthwhile and empowering change will come through being Born Again, Spirit-filled and, by choice, continuing an ever-deepening relationship with God. The only measure that can be used in the desperate needs that humankind faces on the earth today, is to encounter the love, forgiveness and hope that is found in Jesus. You and I were born into sin. The world continues to decay in cancerous sin that is spreading more wildly than man can contain or deal with. The Bible talks about deep darkness covering the earth; and one simply needs to watch news broadcasts to see evidence of the madness that is ever increasing. Believers do, however, have great hope amidst the darkness. God has said that in the darkness, His light will shine, for His Glory will be what clothes those that belong to Him. Even though our physical bodies are ageing, our spirits are being renewed day by day.

'Therefore we do not become discouraged [utterly spiritless, exhausted, and wearied out through fear]. Though our outer man is progressively decaying and wasting away, yet our inner self is being progressively renewed day by day.'
(2 CORINTHIANS 4:16)

Being holy is not an impossibility in this day and age of 'anything goes', the lack of accountability and respect, sexual immorality and devious practices. If living a holy life was impossible in this life, God would never have commanded that we be holy as He is holy. (Lev. 19:2). Living a holy life is living a separated life. Not like a nun or a monk, unless you choose to live that way, but choosing in your heart to live a life that is pleasing to God. It is living a life of faith in Christ on account of what He has done to secure our holiness. Holy living is, quite simply, right living. It is not living in judgement or criticism of those who do not choose to live like you, but rather letting your light shine, so that you can bring light and life into what may seem an endlessly dark tunnel for them.

'Even as [in His love] He chose us, actually picked us out for Himself as His own in Christ before the foundation of the world, that we should be holy (consecrated and set apart for Him) and blameless in His sight, even above reproach, before Him in love.'
(EPHESIANS 1:4 AMP)

My Reflections on Living a Holy Life

You may well have experienced the aftermath of living a lifestyle of unholy practices and bad choices. While the payoff may be pleasurable at the time, it is not permanent. (A cup of pleasure. A sea of pain!) Don't waste your eternity on living for temporal rewards. Today is the day to choose to live a holy and a powerful life through Christ Jesus, and have God's favour on your side.

Women – God's Final Creation ✍

'IT IS NOT GOOD THAT MAN SHOULD BE ALONE; I WILL MAKE HIM A HELPER COMPARABLE TO HIM.'
(GENESIS 2:1)

The beauty of your womanhood. When was the last time you created some 'me time' to simply stop and consider the beauty of your womanhood? Whew! I can hear you saying; create space, take time, what's that? Even now you are feeling guilty for taking this moment to breathe and allow yourself to indulge in a little soul food. Even more so do I encourage you to think about the fact that never before in the history of humanity has there been another you. Never will there be another you! Long after your footprints leave this earth, the only part of you that will remain will be the legacy and the memories you have left behind in the hearts and minds of others. Woman, you are a unique creation. You have been created by God with purpose, passion and with destiny designed in your very DNA. You are the very woman you were designed to be! Not one human being has been born by accident, regardless of their circumstances. You are here because you are born for a time such as this; a time to be transformed by God as He sovereignly uses life's processes to form you and challenge you to grow into that unique woman He had in mind when He first designed you.

Woman was God's final creation. When He created Adam, He saw that His creation was good. But when God made Eve, He looked at her and saw that she was 'very good'. When God saw Adam tending the Garden of Eden, He said,

> *'It is not good that man should be alone; I will*
> *make him a helper comparable to Him.'*
> (GENESIS 2:1)

Note that the woman is comparable to man, not inferior or in any way lesser than a man, and most importantly note that in God's eyes there is no differentiation made between a man and woman, except in the area of physical strength. In all of God's creation, He saw it was good, but that it was incomplete without a woman. God's purpose for the earth being filled with His Glory could not be perpetuated without His creation of the woman. Women are God's instruments for bringing forth life. It was the one woman Mary, who brought forth the life of the Lord Jesus Christ, and He came forever to liberate women and call them to arise to the beauty of their womanhood. Jesus is the original Emancipator. Sadly, in many cultures today, with the horrors of Femicide and genital mutilation still being practised, this liberating message that Jesus came to give has not been given the freedom of acceptance to millions of deserving women. Women have always had a place of appreciation, priority and purpose in the heart of God. The world, however, has had us believe the contrary. We only need to look at the abuse of women worldwide and how women have consistently through the ages been degraded and defiled through the relentless demand for woman and girl-child prostitutes, pornography and sex slavery. Imagine the woman who had been drawing water at the well hearing the Man, Jesus, address her with compassion and respect even though He knew her past and her present circumstances; that she had been married five times and was living with a man that was not her husband. Yet there was no judgement, no rejection, but rather a restoration of the dignity of her womanhood as He displayed His mercy and kindness and showed His love for her despite her past. The woman caught in adultery also experienced powerful life-changing forgiveness and total restoration that only Jesus can give, as He saved her from the punishment of death by stoning. She was redeemed and restored to the beauty of her

Today is yours. Let Him redeem it, redeem you. Now is the time to arise in the beauty of your womanhood. Be free to live abundantly. Seize today. It is the only today you have to be all the woman you were designed to be!

womanhood as Jesus forgave her, accepted her and instructed her to go and sin no more.

'One thing we know about God's loving character is that He never makes a mistake. Nothing is out of His control.'
SUSAN LAFLAM, *SUCCESS FOR WOMEN*

Jesus never takes anything away from us – He only adds to our lives, and then abundantly. God has a very specific plan to restore you to the beauty of your womanhood and to enable you to arise and be everything He created you to be. He desires for you to stand tall even in the midst of your falling world. He wants you to become unshakable, immovable and established, so that through Him, you too can overcome and conquer those areas in your life which constantly threaten to keep you stunted in your growth and restrict you from **standing tall**. Simply ask Him today to set you free in the areas where you need to be liberated. He wants you free more than you want to be free.

From a human perspective Esther would not be the woman chosen to shape a nation. Orphaned at a young age, raised by her cousin Mordecai, and unschooled in the ways of the socialites of her day; yet, God set her aside for a time, brought her into a harem where she was taught the routines and requirements that would best suit the king, and then she was released into her destiny: trained, groomed, prepared, and well adjusted to walk in the position of stateswoman. Her destiny was what she was designed to be. The wife of the king was her role, but her destiny was to be an Ambassador for the Kingdom of God. Her assignment was to arise in the midst of her circumstances and fulfil God's purpose in fearlessly saving the nation of Israel from extinction.

An ambassador is a representative of a kingdom who ranks in the highest office on behalf of her country. She must know the country's affairs, current issues, policies, plans and strategies. A stateswoman must be proactive and in-the-know in order to act swiftly, and speak accurately and with authority. From orphan to stateswoman,

Esther became the most powerful woman in her day (Esther 9:29). Interestingly, the Oxford Dictionary's definition of an ambassador is a servant [Latin]. It was Esther's attitude to serving that elevated her to the position and ability to save. What roles of service are you being called to that may well lead to a call to save the lives, the situation or the future of others?

> *'How lovely to think that no one need wait a moment,*
> *we can start now, start slowly changing the world!'*
> ANNE FRANK, *THE DIARY OF ANNE FRANK*

As we look at the happenings in our fatigued world, it is easy to become discouraged, to lose our joy and strength, and perhaps at times, even our faith. But it is:

> *'...for a time such as this that God has*
> *brought you into His Kingdom'*
> (ESTHER 4:4)

As you take time to draw deeply from the well of your salvation with joy, and recognize that God has placed a call on you to play the part that only you can play in the extension of His Kingdom here on earth, yield your life to God in thanksgiving and let God clothe you with His ambassadorial robes of authority and purpose, and let Him place on you His mantle, His imprint, that represents His Kingdom and reflects His Glory to those around you. When Esther had done her part in taking responsibility for her position and was obedient to the call to play her role in pleading with the king on behalf of the Jewish nation, God released His Sovereignty and gave her the power to decree protection and salvation to her land. And so it is with each one of us who have been born into His Kingdom. Let us arise in humility under the mighty hand of God and in due season we will be exalted. Arise and be united to impact the people of your nation, the people of the world, and play your part to bring renewal, regeneration and restoration to a very weary world.

As God grooms His women to fulfil the ambassadorial role for His Kingdom, He extends great measures of His grace towards us. I am ever grateful that in the frailty of our humanity, He entrusts us with so much. Whatever role we fulfil in His Kingdom, His higher call is for Jesus to be reflected in us. We reflect the Son when the fires of purification have burnt within, much like silver that has been purified many times. We can only share with others with integrity when we are real in our humanity; when the masks have been removed and we know that His grace is at its strongest when we admit that He is our greatest need. In knowing that our deepest need is to trust God, the challenge then calls for us to endure those processes that build character on the inside to match the ambassadorial robes displayed on the outside. We can have all the exterior adornments and totally deface them if our character cannot nobly stand in the day of criticism, temptation and persecution. The more you desire God to work through you, the more character-building we will have to go through! As long as we are alive to God, we will constantly have to withstand and reject circumstances that would try to disfigure our reflection of Him. It is worth remembering '*that God always causes us to triumph in Christ Jesus*' *(2 Corinthians 2:14)*.

We can only minister in integrity when we are real in our humanity.

Psalm 44 reveals some of the processes God will take you through as He grooms you to fulfil the role of being His ambassador.

Spiritual warfare forms part of the role of any woman that belongs to God and for His ambassadors throughout the ages. However, Jesus is the mighty One and He has defeated our foes with His Sword of authority, truth and humility. We can bask in the afterglow of His triumphant victory. An ambassador has authority but has no grounds for arrogance. When we present ourselves to receive our ambassadorial assignment we must come in humility. Then He shall guide us to do tremendous things. God's

God's power knows no limits.

power knows no limits. Even the greatest of foes that would rise against you can be resisted by the power of God. The heart is the harbour of the intents of man. When intentions of evil are arrayed against you, God will pierce the hearts of your enemies so their evil intentions become lifeless; void of power to harm you. Esther could have faced certain death for entering the king's chambers unannounced, but the king's sceptre was extended forth for the saving of her life and for freedom of speech. The sceptre of God's Kingdom is continually extended towards you and if you will embrace His righteousness and hate wickedness you will experience the fullness of righteousness, peace and joy in this life. As a daughter of the King you shall be overwhelmed with the favour you receive. God's intimacy takes you into the inner part of His palace – the deep places of His heart. In His Presence you are enrobed with the richest of clothes, inwrought with gold, which is symbolic of your faith that has been refined in the fire.

God's desire for you is to leave a rich legacy for the generations that will follow; a people, who because of your legacy, will praise and give God thanks forever and ever.

My Reflections on Being
a Woman of Great Worth

A Chosen Vessel 🌹

In this day of self-and-other-idolization, the stockpiling of material possessions, the amassing of brand names to overburdened debt proportions, and the frenzied ambition to be 'famous' at all costs, it is sobering to remember how frail the world of the glitterati is. It is often among the Hollywood hype that we have to acknowledge that it can, at times, be a world that is indeed falling. The media is masterful at divulging who the next poor victim of rehabilitation or arrest is. 'Look at me, look at me', the pictures scream. But when the world looks at them 24/7, that kind of intense interest becomes too much to bear.

True promotion comes from the Lord. The problem for us with this concept, however, is that when it doesn't happen within our time frame, we are more than tempted to get out there and create it ourselves. Timing is everything. Timing has to do with character development and many times when we step out in our own 'world of glitterati', blowing our own trumpets and raising our own fanfare, we are out there before our character is strong and resistant enough to ride out the demands that come with unbridled ambition.

In my role as a speaker and facilitator, I meet many people who are burnt out, wrung out, and spun out, because they thought they could go it alone. It's a tough old world out there and if God is not with you in something, it can produce great anxiety, a debt-burden, and even grave disappointment – not a great reward for all your efforts to be 'somebody'.

We can learn much from the allegory of the 'Chosen Vessel'. Unfortunately the author is

> *Don't copy the behaviour and customs of this world, but let God transform you into a new person by changing the way you think. Then you will know what God wants you to do, and you will know how good and pleasing and perfect His will really is.*
>
> (ROMANS 12:12 NLT)

unknown, but I have no doubt that the writer of this piece walked the path that allowed him or her to know that we are most effective and **standing tall** when we are available, willing and graced with humility.

A Chosen Vessel

The Master was searching for a vessel to use
Before Him were many, which one would He choose?
'Take me' cried the gold one. 'I'm shiny and bright,
I am of great value, and I do things just right.
My beauty and lustre will outshine the rest,
And for someone like You, Master, gold would be best.'

The Master passed on with no word at all,
and looked at a silver urn, narrow and tall.
'I'll serve you dear Master I'll pour out
Your wine, I'll be on your table, whenever you dine.
My lines are so graceful, my carvings so true,
And silver will certainly complement You.'

Unheeding the Master passed on to the Vessel of brass;
Wide-mouthed and shallow and polished like glass.
'Here, here' cried the vessel. 'I know I will do,
Place me on your table for all men to view.'
'Look at me' called the goblet of crystal so clear,
'Though fragile am I, I will serve you with fear.'

The Master came next to the vessel of wood
Polished and carved it solidly stood,
'You may use me Master,' the wooden bowl said
'But I'd rather you used me for fruit, not bread.'

Then the Master looked down on the vessel of clay,
Empty and broken it helplessly lay.
No hope had the vessel that the Master might choose
to cleanse and make whole, to fill and to use.

Oh this is the vessel I've been hoping to find,
I'll mend it and use it and make it all mine.

I'll need not the vessel with pride of itself,
Nor one that's narrow to sit on the shelf.
Nor one that is big-mouthed and shallow and loud,
Nor one that displays its contents so proud.

Then gently He lifted the vessel of clay
Mended and cleansed it and filled it that day.
Spoke to it kindly – there's work you must do.
Just pour out to others as I pour into you.

Bending down to help someone else is the tallest thing you can do. Benjamin Disraeli, a British statesman and literary figure, made the following statement: *'The greatest good you can do for another is not just to share your riches, but to reveal to him his own.'* **Standing tall** is about being the person God created you to be. God has absolutely nothing against you being prosperous. His Word is, in fact, full of His desire for you to prosper, live a life of abundance, and be successful in everything you do. He does, however, have an issue with pride!

'To fear the Lord is to hate evil;
I hate pride and arrogance, evil
behaviour and perverse speech.'
(PROVERBS 8:13, NIV)

It's a long and lonely road when all we have accomplished in life is money, branded items and a haughty attitude, especially since we leave this earth as naked as we came in. The only legacy or real value will be what you have built into the lives of others. How will they remember you and will your legacy outlive and outlast you? Live your life as a shining example, so that when you leave your legacy it will shine forever.

The greatest good you can do for another is not just to share your riches, but to reveal to him his own.
BENJAMIN DISRAELI

My Reflections on Being a Chosen Vessel

❖ When last did you say, 'Here I am Lord, send me?' Perhaps today is the day!

❖ Who can you 'pour into' today? Where can you make the most contribution today?

❖ What will the history book of your life say about you?

My Reflections

My Reflections

My Reflections

.

ABOUT THE AUTHOR

Angelique du Toit is a businesswoman, a life-transformation speaker, a seminar facilitator and an author of substance and style who encourages people to live with greater purpose, passion and productivity in a meaningful, inspirational and instantly applicable way. Having no high school education, Angelique was equipped only with what everyone else in life has – the power of choice! She turned what seemed a dead-end road into an opportunity to crown her life, her business and her future with abundant success, and now she can do the same for you!

Everything you need to be successful is already inside of you, and Angelique's expertise will help to take you to the place you deserve to be. Internal transformation is the key to having powerful external impact, and the multitudes of successful people that Angelique has spoken to over the years have all been equipped and empowered to implement life strategies and principles to live victoriously. Shaping hearts, shifting minds and sharing success across every spectrum of your life is what Angelique shares with you.

After being involved in the wonderful world of direct selling for nearly three decades, in 1999 Angelique started her own personal and professional development company, Women Arise. She has the privilege of being the co-owner and director of Annique Health and Beauty, a proudly South African company with a 45-year legacy. Angelique believes that in life, your business and your future, 'You win or lose by the way that YOU choose!'

angeldt@iafrica.com
www.angeliquedutoit.co.za